Natural
Harry

Natural Harry

Delicious plant-based
summer recipes

Harriet Birrell

Photographed by Nikole Ramsay

Hardie Grant

BOOKS

Contents

Introduction

If you take one retro wooden caravan, two passionate people, a truckload of organic ingredients and blend it all together, what do you get? Natural Harry.

Natural Harry started as a pipe dream. We wanted to build a 1950s-inspired wooden van serving vibrant, nourishing, organic smoothies and raw desserts. Determined to do just that, Fraser and I began building the van in midwinter 2013. With his carpentry talent and passion for bespoke design, Fraser handcrafted this little gem from scratch. Our pipe dream was real!

By the summer of 2013, Natural Harry had wheels and rolled on happily into our seaside town of Barwon Heads. Our van sat on a leafy vacant block in the main street of town. Hoisted umbrellas, scattered beanbags and cruisy tunes set the tone for a relaxed, sunny summer's pit-stop.

What started as a beachside smoothie van has grown. Natural Harry shows you another way to think about food. This book includes more than 70 delicious plant-based recipes. The food might look naughty but it is just plain nice. The focus is on nutrition and quality ingredients.

Thriving on a plant-based diet can be simple. Including more wholefoods in your diet can improve your skin, digestion, energy levels, and help with weight management.

The recipes for our most popular smoothies and raw desserts from the Natural Harry caravan are featured, as well as vibrant breakfast bowls, savoury breakfast ideas, fresh summer salads, warm dinners and delectable desserts for a balmy evening. I have also included recipes for my favourite easy-to-make basics that add extra flavour to any dish.

You can easily source most of the ingredients used in these recipes from your local organic grocer or farmers' market. Some recipes include special ingredients, such as maqui berry powder or cacao nibs, to add a bit of a kick. You can find more information about them on page 164.

I am so excited to share with you my favourite fresh and simple plant-based recipes. All of my recipes are free of meat, dairy and egg, with no refined sugar or gluten. It is not about what might be missing in these recipes; this book is about celebrating the amazing abundance of whole, fresh, colourful plant foods we have available, and the simply delicious, nourishing dishes you can create with them.

Harry
x

Tips for a
plant-based lifestyle

EQUIPMENT

- Chemical-free non-stick pots and pans
- Glass jars with lids
- Metal or glass straws
- Springform cake tins
- Silicone slice and cupcake moulds
- Vegetable spiraliser
- High-speed blender
- Food processor

SHOPPING

I recommend shopping at your local organic fruit and vegetable store or farmers' market for all your fresh produce. This will not only ensure great quality, but you are also encouraging local businesses. Farmers' markets are also generally better value and a lovely ritual you can feel good about.

GROW YOUR OWN

Plant in spring to be ready for summer. Leafy greens and herbs are especially easy to grow and are perfect ingredients to have on hand to add to a green smoothie or fresh salad. Some herbs and vegetables that grow well in summer include:

New Zealand spinach	cucumber	basil
silverbeet (Swiss chard)	tomatoes	parsley
cos (romaine) lettuce	peas	dill
rocket (arugula)	zucchini (courgette)	thyme
celery	oregano	coriander (cilantro)
eggplant (aubergine)	mint	

LOOK AFTER YOURSELF

With so much information out there about conflicting studies, programs, regimens, routines and quick fixes it can be easy to lose sight of the bigger picture, don't you think?

No one is perfect. We all live in the real world and no one is 'holier than thou'. We can simply do our best.

I believe a healthy, happy life is built on solid foundations and good habits. It doesn't have to be complicated. Here are my fundamentals for a healthy day:

Eat	**Move**
more wholefoods, fruits and vegetables, nuts, seeds, grains and legumes.	your body daily. Walk, swim, do yoga, surf, join a team, have fun.
Drink	**Play**
around 8 glasses or 2 litres (68 fl oz) of water per day.	and be silly, laugh a lot.
Sleep	**Be still**
– get enough. Listen to your body.	for 2 minutes a day. Sit and breathe deeply.

STAY CONNECTED

Spread the word and be inspired. Share your plant-based recipe creations by using the hashtag #naturalharry

Website: www.naturalharry.com.au

Instagram: @natural_harry

Facebook: www.facebook.com/naturalharry

Smoothie tips

- Buy fresh produce in bulk. It is cheaper during its peak season. Stock up on your staple smoothie items when available. Freeze diced mango, pineapple, banana, berries and apple in zip-lock bags or airtight containers for ready-to-go smoothie ingredients.

- Wait for fruit to ripen. This improves the texture and taste of your smoothies. Ripened fruit is more easily assimilated by the body, reducing digestive issues caused by starchy, unripened fruit.

- Dice and freeze cucumber to have on hand as a cleansing, nutrient-dense alternative to ice.

- Add frozen banana and/or mango to smoothies to make them thicker and creamier.

- Rinse your blender jug immediately after making a smoothie. This makes it much easier to clean.

- Pour leftover smoothie mixture into popsicle moulds and freeze for a ready-made healthy snack on a hot day.

SMOOTHIES

MAQUI BERRY &
PASSIONFRUIT SMOOTHIE

As far as making something a bit 'fancy pants' with little effort goes, this one is the ticket. It's a sure-fire crowd-pleaser. Its vibrant colour and vital nutrients will leave you feeling energised and ready for a fun-filled beach day.

Serves 2
Prep time: 5 minutes

SMOOTHIE

4 large ripe passionfruit

3 frozen bananas, cut into chunks

65 g (2¼ oz/½ cup) blueberries, fresh or
    frozen

1 tablespoon maqui berry powder

½ teaspoon vanilla powder

375 ml (12½ fl oz/1½ cups) almond milk

TO SERVE

2 teaspoons coconut flakes (optional)

Cut the passionfruit in half and spoon the pulp into the bottom of two glasses. Blend all the remaining smoothie ingredients until smooth and pour over the passionfruit. Top with a sprinkling of coconut flakes, if desired, and serve.

COOKIES & CREAM
SMOOTHIE

Who doesn't love that magic combo of cookies and cream? And for brekkie? Even better. Using frozen bananas makes this smoothie even creamier and more delicious.

Serves 2
Prep time: 5 minutes

SMOOTHIE

4 frozen bananas, cut into chunks

1 tablespoon cacao nibs

2 teaspoons coconut sugar

1 teaspoon vanilla powder

375 ml (12½ fl oz/1½ cups) almond milk
   or other plant-based milk

TO SERVE

3 teaspoons cacao nibs (optional)

2 teaspoons coconut flakes (optional)

In a blender, pulse all the smoothie ingredients a few times to evenly combine, then blend until smooth. You will still be able to see speckles of cacao nibs. Pour the mixture into two glasses.

Sprinkle cacao nibs and coconut flakes over the smoothies, if desired, then serve with a spoon or metal straw.

GREEN WARRIOR
SMOOTHIE

Liquid gold anyone? Not only do you get the alkalising and energising benefits of the fresh fruit and veggies in this smoothie, the citrus juice aids in the absorption of iron from the leafy greens. Make yours super chilled by using at least one frozen ingredient and enjoy it first thing on a balmy summer's morning with the sun on your face.

Serves 2
Prep time: 5 minutes

SMOOTHIE

2 large mangoes, peeled and pitted

1 large green apple, cored and diced

60 g (2 oz) diced frozen cucumber

2 handfuls baby English spinach leaves

2 tablespoons freshly squeezed lemon or lime juice

1 teaspoon super green powder of choice (optional), such as chlorella

375 ml (12½ fl oz/1½ cups) coconut water or purified water

In a blender, process all the ingredients until smooth. Serve immediately.

SKIN GLOW
SMOOTHIE

Quenching and cleansing, like a big drink of water for your skin, this smoothie is chock-a-block full of all the hydrating and free-radical fighting vitamins and minerals your skin craves. It is a powerhouse of antioxidants, tangy, sweet and clean-tasting. Enjoying this smoothie is a delightful way to nourish yourself from the inside out.

Serves 2
Prep time: 5 minutes

SMOOTHIE

130 g (4½ oz/1 cup) mixed berries, fresh or frozen

1 frozen banana, cut into chunks

1 mango cheek, peeled

50 g (1¾ oz/½ cup) cucumber, diced

50 g (1¾ oz/½ cup) pineapple, peeled and diced

10 fresh mint leaves

1 tablespoon freshly squeezed lime juice

1 tablespoon acai powder (optional)

375 ml (12½ fl oz/1½ cups) coconut water or purified water

TO SERVE

small handful of berries (optional)

2 fresh mint sprigs (optional)

In a blender, pulse all the smoothie ingredients to combine, then blend until smooth. To serve, sprinkle with a few berries and top with a mint sprig, if desired.

FROSTED FRUIT
SMOOTHIE

There is something about this combination that is so refreshing you will want to jump into your mason jar. This is my go-to pick-me-up on a scorching summer's afternoon. Use a few pieces of frozen fruit for that extra chill factor.

Serves 2
Prep time: 5 minutes

SMOOTHIE
2 large mangoes, peeled and pitted

200 g (7 oz) pineapple, fresh or frozen, diced

2 tablespoons fresh mint leaves

375 ml (12½ fl oz/1½ cups) coconut water or purified water

TO SERVE
2 fresh mint sprigs (optional)

In a blender, pulse all the smoothie ingredients to combine, then blend until smooth. Pour into tall glasses and top with a mint sprig, if desired. Serve immediately.

CACAO-BUNGA (dude) SMOOTHIE

This delicious creamy smoothie will give you bucketloads of energy to kickstart your day - just like those infamous 90s reptiles had. It tastes like mocha ice cream, only it's full of antioxidants, vitamins and minerals. Ninja Turtle outfit optional.

Serves 2
Prep time: 5 minutes

SMOOTHIE

4 frozen bananas, cut into chunks

2 teaspoons coconut sugar

2 teaspoons cacao powder

½ teaspoon vanilla powder

2 tablespoons organic cold-drip coffee (optional)

375 ml (12½ fl oz/1½ cups) coconut milk or other plant-based milk

TO SERVE

2 teaspoons coconut flakes (optional)

1 teaspoon coffee beans

2 teaspoons cacao nibs

Place all the smoothie ingredients in a blender and blend until smooth. Sprinkle with coconut flakes and coffee beans, or cacao nibs, and enjoy.

CREAMY GREEN
APPLE SMOOTHIE

This smoothie has a creamy texture and a refreshing, slightly tart flavour.
I love how simple it is to prepare, yet how satisfying and sustaining it
is for a busy day ahead. It is also bursting with fibre, healthy fats and
a good dose of vitamin C.

Serves 2
Prep time: 5 minutes

SMOOTHIE

3 large green apples, cored and diced,
   plus apple slices to garnish (optional)
1 large avocado, peeled and stone
   removed
1 small handful diced frozen cucumber
   or ice
2 tablespoons freshly squeezed lime juice
1 tablespoon maple syrup (optional)
375 ml (12½ fl oz/1½ cups) coconut water

In a blender, process all the ingredients
until smooth. Garnish with apple slices,
if desired, and serve immediately.

BREAKFAST

TAKE-AWAY
BREAKFAST JAR

I first made this jar of goodness when Fraser and I needed a yummy and sustaining breakfast during the early summer mornings setting up our little caravan. It is all about the balance of crunchy elements and smooth, creamy textures. Don't forget to take a spoon with you!

Serves 2
Prep time: 10 minutes (+ soaking overnight)

CHIA PUDDING

500 ml (17 fl oz/2 cups) almond milk
  or coconut milk
85 g (3 oz/½ cup) chia seeds
½ teaspoon vanilla powder

LAYERS

80 g (2¾ oz) Rainbow raw-nola
  (page 140)
225 g (8 oz/¾ cup) Maqui berry & lime
  chia jam (page 142)
100 g (3½ oz) Coconut yoghurt
  (page 144)
2 green apples, cored and julienned

Combine all the chia pudding ingredients in a large jar or bowl and stir well. Leave to stand for 10 minutes before stirring once more. Place in the refrigerator overnight.

In the morning, layer the chia pudding, raw-nola and jam in a small glass jar, then top it off with coconut yoghurt and julienned apple. Pop a lid on it and Bob's your uncle!

CREAMY BLUEBERRY
SMOOTHIE BOWL

This is such a great way to use your homemade coconut yoghurt.
The texture of this breakfast bowl is so creamy and delicious. It's full
of fibre and good energy to keep you going all morning. Try making this
one with your favourite summer berries.

Serves 2
Prep time: 5 minutes

SMOOTHIE
4 frozen bananas, cut into chunks
130 g (4½ oz/1 cup) fresh or frozen
   blueberries
240 g (12 oz/1 cup) Coconut yoghurt
   (page 144) or coconut milk

TOPPINGS
20 g (¾ oz/⅓ cup) coconut flakes
2 tablespoons pistachio nuts, lightly
   crushed
¼ cup fresh or frozen raspberries

Combine all the smoothie ingredients in
a blender. Pulse several times to combine,
then blend until smooth. You may have to
use a tamper to aid this process. Scoop
out into two bowls and sprinkle generously
with the toppings. Voilà!

MAQUI & ACAI
RAINBOW BOWL

There is nothing better than a refreshing and filling smoothie bowl to begin your day on a warm summer's morning. This is my favourite combination. This creamy, tangy mango purée and antioxidant-packed superfood smoothie is a delicious contrast to the crunchy toppings. Sprinkle a little of the toppings into the bottom of the bowls before filling for a yummy surprise at the end.

Serves 2
Prep time: 10 minutes

MANGO PURÉE
2 mangoes, peeled and pitted
1 tablespoon freshly squeezed lime juice
125 ml (4 fl oz/½ cup) coconut water

SMOOTHIE
130 g (4½ oz/1 cup) frozen mixed berries
4 frozen bananas, cut into chunks
2 tablespoons freshly squeezed lime juice
1 tablespoon acai powder
1 tablespoon maqui berry powder
375 ml (12½ fl oz/1½ cups) coconut water

TOPPINGS
210 g (7½ oz/1½ cups) Rainbow raw-nola
    (page 140)
1 tablespoon coconut flakes
2 fresh mint sprigs (optional)

In a blender, pulse all the mango purée ingredients to combine, then blend until smooth. Divide between two bowls, then rinse out the blender jug.

Repeat this process for the smoothie ingredients. Pour into the centre of the mango purée in the bowls, then top with rainbow raw-nola, coconut flakes and a sprig of mint, if desired. Enjoy in the sunshine.

TROPPO
BREKKIE BOWL

Made with all things tropical, this bowl of creamy goodness is like a scrumptious slice of tropical island life. I like to make mine when I have a leftover coconut, as the shell makes two perfect little bowls.

Serves 2
Prep time: 2 minutes

MANGO SAUCE
3 mangoes, peeled and pitted
juice of 1 lime
1 tablespoon coconut water

BOWL
90 g (3 oz/1 cup) desiccated (shredded)
   coconut
240 g (12 oz/1 cup) Coconut yoghurt
   (page 144)
2 ripe bananas, peeled and sliced

TO SERVE
2 lime wedges
2 tablespoons desiccated (shredded)
   coconut (optional)

In a blender, process the mango sauce ingredients until smooth.

Divide the desiccated coconut between two bowls. Layer the coconut yoghurt, mango sauce and sliced bananas on top of the coconut. Serve with a wedge of fresh lime and desiccated coconut, if desired.

MANGO & BERRY
CHIA PUDDING

On their own, chia seeds do not hold a lot of flavour, but they are packed full of important nutrients that the body loves. They are filling and sustaining and, when combined with other nutritionally dense and tasty ingredients, they transform into an amazing pudding that is super easy to prepare and so delicious. This creamy breakfast pudding is just that.

Serves 2
Prep time: 10 minutes (+ soaking overnight)

PUDDING

750 ml (25½ fl oz/3 cups) coconut milk

170 g (6 oz/1 cup) chia seeds

3 mango cheeks, peeled and diced

½ teaspoon vanilla powder

TOPPINGS

360 (12½ oz/1½ cups) Coconut yoghurt
  (page 144)

130 g (4½ oz/1 cup) mixed berries,
  fresh or frozen

1 mango cheek, peeled and diced

Combine all the pudding ingredients in a large jar or bowl and stir well. Leave to stand for 10 minutes before stirring once more. Place in the refrigerator overnight.

In the morning, divide the pudding between two medium bowls (or jars if you are taking breakfast away). Top with coconut yoghurt, then sprinkle with the mixed berries and mango pieces.

TOAST TOPPINGS
5 WAYS

Creating a nourishing cafe-style brekkie at home doesn't have to be time-consuming. These delicious toast toppings give you all the satisfying quality ingredients without the fuss. They're perfect to enjoy after a beautiful Sunday beach stroll or as a quick and healthy weekday breakfast.

AVO SMASH WITH BEETROOT RELISH

Serves 2
Prep time: 5 minutes
Cook time: 5 minutes

Clockwise from top:

Avo smash with beetroot relish
Cashew 'cheese' with minty pea mash
Fancy pants PB & J
Thyme mushrooms & hummus
Roasted capsicum & hummus

1 large ripe avocado, peeled and
   stone removed
1 lime, quartered
4 slices quality gluten-free bread
2 tablespoons Healthy-mite spread
   (page 124)
80 g (2¾ oz) Beetroot & dill
   relish (page 122)

TO SERVE
5 g (¼ oz/¼ cup) fresh dill sprigs
   (optional)
lime wedges

In a bowl, mash the avocado with a fork. Squeeze half of the lime over it and stir the juice in.

Toast the bread slices and spread each with the healthy-mite. Divide the smashed avocado over the four pieces of toast and top each with a tablespoon of beetroot relish. Sprinkle with a few dill sprigs, if desired, and serve with a wedge of lime.

CASHEW 'CHEESE' WITH MINTY PEA MASH

Serves 2
Prep time: 5 minutes
Cook time: 15 minutes

180 g (6½ oz/1½ cups) fresh or
    frozen peas
5 g (¼ oz/¼ cup) fresh mint leaves,
    plus extra to serve
½ medium avocado, peeled and
    stone removed
4 slices quality gluten-free bread
80 g (2¾ oz) Garlic & chive cashew
    cream 'cheese' (page 130)
1 pinch quality mineral salt

TO SERVE
lime wedges

Cover the peas and mint with water in a saucepan and bring to the boil. Reduce the heat and simmer for 10 minutes. Drain and set aside.

Mash the avocado with a fork. Lightly stir in the peas and mint.

Toast the bread until golden. Spread each slice with a tablespoon of garlic and chive cashew cream 'cheese', then top with the minty pea mash. Scatter a few fresh mint leaves and a pinch of salt over each slice and serve with a wedge of lime.

FANCY PANTS PB & J

Serves 2
Prep time: 5 minutes

4 slices quality gluten-free bread
140 g (5 oz) Maqui berry & lime chia jam
    (page 142)
80 g (2¾ oz) natural peanut butter
2 tablespoons coconut flakes
seeds of 1 pomegranate

Toast the bread slices until golden. Layer each with a tablespoon of chia jam and peanut butter, then sprinkle with coconut flakes. Sprinkle on a generous amount of pomegranate seeds.

THYME MUSHROOMS & HUMMUS

Serves 2
Prep time: 5 minutes
Cook time: 15 minutes

270 g (9½ oz/3 cups) button
  mushrooms, sliced
1 tablespoon tamari
2 teaspoons fresh thyme leaves
120 g (4½ oz/4 cups) baby English spinach
2 garlic cloves, peeled and finely chopped
4 slices quality gluten-free bread
120 g (4½ oz) Paprika & capsicum
  hummus (page 138)

TO SERVE
2 tablespoons Almond dukkah (page 126)
2 tablespoons fresh thyme leaves

Heat two non-stick frying pans. Add the mushrooms, tamari and thyme to one. Sauté the mushrooms on medium heat until cooked through. Add the spinach and garlic to the other pan and sauté until just wilted.

Toast the bread slices and spread each piece with a tablespoon of the hummus. Spoon the spinach on top and scatter the mushrooms over the spinach. Sprinkle with the dukkah and fresh thyme leaves.

ROASTED CAPSICUM & HUMMUS

Serves 2
Prep time: 5 minutes
Cook time: 30 minutes

1 large red capsicum (bell pepper),
  halved and seeds removed
4 slices quality gluten-free bread
120 g (4½ oz) Roasted garlic & rosemary
  hummus (page 136)
1 tablespoon pea shoots
1 tablespoon cold-pressed olive oil

Preheat the oven to 200°C (390°F) fan-forced.

Place the capsicum on a baking tray lined with baking paper and bake for 25 minutes, or until lightly charred.

Toast the bread slices until golden and spread each with a tablespoon of hummus.

Slice the cooked capsicum into strips and lay it over the toast. Sprinkle with pea shoots and drizzle with the olive oil. Serve immediately.

MAINS

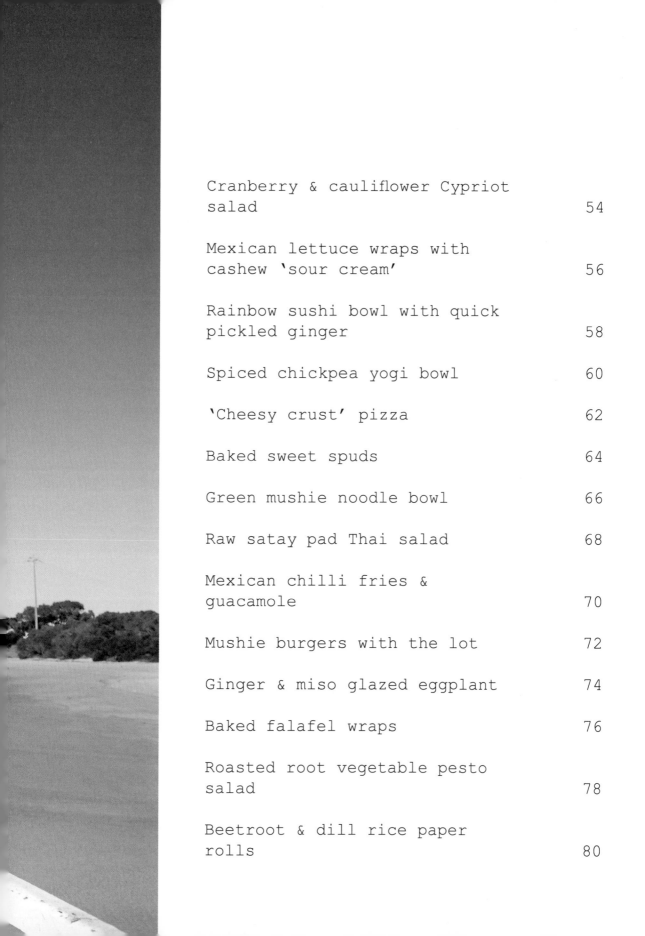

CRANBERRY & CAULIFLOWER CYPRIOT SALAD

This is my plant-based and grain-free take on the much-loved Cypriot salad. It holds all the flavour and texture of the original with even more goodness. Freekeh has been replaced with clever cauliflower 'rice', dairy Greek yoghurt with a delicious minty tahini dressing, and currants with sweet, tart cranberries.

Serves 2
Prep time: 25 minutes
Cook time: 5 minutes

SALAD
80 g (2¾ oz/½ cup) almonds

70 g (2½ oz/½ cup) pine nuts

250 g (9 oz/1½ cups) tinned brown lentils, drained and rinsed

180 g (6½ oz/1½ cups) dried cranberries

60 ml (2 fl oz/¼ cup) freshly squeezed lemon juice

60 g (2 oz/2 cups) coriander (cilantro) leaves

60 g (2 oz/2 cups) flat-leaf (Italian) parsley

1 red onion, thinly sliced

2 tablespoons baby capers

⅛ teaspoon quality mineral salt

seeds of 1 pomegranate

CAULIFLOWER 'RICE'
½ head (approx. 420 g/15 oz) cauliflower, stalk removed

140 g (5 oz/1 cup) cashew nuts

1 teaspoon sesame oil

DRESSING
255 g (9 oz/1 cup) Mint tahini dressing (page 132)

1 teaspoon ground cumin (optional)

1 fresh mint sprig (optional)

For the salad, toast the almonds and pine nuts in a non-stick frying pan over medium heat, stirring for 5 minutes, or until browned. Once cooled slightly, crush the nuts. Set aside.

For the cauliflower 'rice', cut the cauliflower into eight pieces and pulse in a food processor with the cashew nuts and sesame oil until a rice-like texture is achieved. Place the cauliflower 'rice' in a large mixing bowl and top with the remaining salad ingredients, except the pomegranate seeds. Toss until evenly combined.

Sprinkle the pomegranate seeds over the salad.

Serve with a bowl of mint tahini dressing on the side, sprinkled with ground cumin and topped with a few fresh mint leaves, if desired.

MEXICAN LETTUCE WRAPS WITH CASHEW 'SOUR CREAM'

These super-fresh lettuce wraps are the perfect clean, crisp and healthy finger food. The cos lettuce provides just the right amount of crunch, and the colourful contents are a delicious tangy, sweet and savoury mix. I love to have a batch ready when we have people over and they also double as a fun recipe to get the kids involved.

Serves 4
Prep time: 20 minutes (+ 3 hours soaking)

SALAD MIXTURE
500 g (1 lb 2 oz/3 cups) mango flesh, diced
400 g (14 oz) tomatoes, diced
2 large avocados, peeled, stones removed, diced
20 g (¾ oz/¼ cup) spring onion (scallion), thinly sliced
1 medium red chilli, seeded and thinly sliced
5 g (¼ oz/¼ cup) coriander (cilantro) leaves, chopped
juice of 1 lime

CASHEW 'SOUR CREAM'
140 g (5 oz/1 cup) raw cashew nuts, soaked for 3 hours or overnight, drained and rinsed
125 ml (4 fl oz/½ cup) purified water
2 teaspoons freshly squeezed lemon juice
1 teaspoon apple-cider vinegar
½ teaspoon quality mineral salt

TO SERVE
2 large cos (romaine) lettuces, leaves separated and washed
coriander (cilantro) leaves

Combine all the salad ingredients in a bowl and pour over the lime juice. Gently fold the mixture together until evenly combined.

For the cashew 'sour cream', pulse all the ingredients in a blender to combine, then blend until smooth.

Fill each cos leaf with a generous amount of the salad mixture and a dollop of cashew 'sour cream'. Sprinkle the lettuce wraps with extra coriander to serve.

RAINBOW SUSHI BOWL WITH QUICK PICKLED GINGER

This nourishing open sushi bowl provides a whole spectrum of vibrant foods. It has become a regular meal in our household, as it never ceases to satisfy and is always fun to prepare. We have found incorporating more colourful raw fruit and vegetables into our diet works to nourish us from the inside out, improving clarity in skin and eyes, strengthening nails and hair, healing and improving digestion, and increasing energy and hydration.

Serves 2
Prep time: 20 minutes

QUICK PICKLED GINGER
20 g (¾ oz/¼ cup) fresh ginger, peeled and thinly sliced
2 tablespoons apple-cider vinegar
1½ tablespoons coconut sugar

CAULIFLOWER 'RICE'
½ head (approx. 420 g/15 oz) cauliflower, stalk removed
140 g (5 oz/1 cup) cashew nuts
1 teaspoon sesame oil

SALAD
30 g (1 oz/1 cup) baby English spinach
1 medium carrot, sliced into ribbons
1 red capsicum (bell pepper), sliced
1 yellow capsicum (bell pepper), sliced
1 large avocado, peeled, stone removed, diced
2 sheets yaki nori, or sushi seaweed, shredded
80 g (2¾ oz) Beetroot & ginger sauerkraut (page 134)

TO SERVE
2 teaspoons black or white sesame seeds
1 tablespoon tamari (optional)
2 teaspoons chopped fresh chives (optional)

For the quick pickled ginger, combine all the ingredients in a bowl. Stir well and set aside.

For the cauliflower 'rice', cut the cauliflower into eight pieces. Place in a food processor with the cashew nuts and sesame oil and pulse eight to ten times to an even, grainy, rice-like texture. Divide between two small bowls and place the bowls in the centre of two larger plates.

Arrange the salad ingredients in sections around the outside of the bowls and sprinkle the cauliflower 'rice' with the sesame seeds and quick pickled ginger, using a little of the liquid from the pickled ginger as a dressing.

Serve with a small dish of tamari and chives, if desired.

*Tip: Squeeze lemon or lime juice over your sliced avocado to slow the oxidisation process – it will keep the avocado from turning brown.

SPICED CHICKPEA
YOGI BOWL

I love to have big batches of sauerkraut and hummus ready to add to rainbow salad bowls like this one for a fast and healthy lunch. Growing a variety of herbs and leafy greens is another great way to have fresh salad ingredients available all the time. It is always fun playing with different combinations. I find these spiced chickpeas are a quick and tasty way to add some hearty nourishment as well.

Serves 2
Prep time: 15 minutes
Cook time: 10 minutes

SPICED CHICKPEAS

1 teaspoon ground cumin

2 teaspoons smoked paprika

½ teaspoon quality mineral salt

2 teaspoons coconut sugar

1 tablespoon water

500 g (1 lb 2 oz) tinned chickpeas, drained and rinsed

SALAD

300 g (10½ oz/1 cup) Beetroot & mint hummus (page 139)

200 g (7 oz/1 cup) Apple & dill sauerkraut (page 134)

1 large avocado, peeled, stone removed, sliced

120 g (4½ oz/4 cups) rocket (arugula)

TO SERVE

1 tablespoon chopped fresh chives

5 g (¼ oz/¼ cup) fresh dill, stalks removed

1 tablespoon fresh mint leaves

1 fresh lime, quartered

For the spiced chickpeas, put the cumin, paprika, mineral salt, coconut sugar and water in a large bowl and stir into a paste. Add the chickpeas and toss until evenly coated.

Heat a non-stick frying pan over medium heat and transfer the coated chickpeas to the pan. Stir until the chickpeas are evenly coated, lightly browned and no liquid remains.

Divide the salad ingredients between two bowls and add the chickpeas. Sprinkle with the fresh herbs and a squeeze of lime.

'CHEESY CRUST' PIZZA

I cannot imagine life without pizza, especially the delicious wood-fired variety. It is such a scrumptious summer meal to enjoy with friends and family. I love to prepare all the ingredients in advance and then let everyone create their own as a fuss-free meal to enjoy together. My favourite pizza is this 100 per cent plant-based version that will leave you feeling energised and satisfied.

Makes 2 small pizzas
Prep time: 25 minutes
Cook time: 30 minutes

BASE
450 g (1 lb/3 cups) sweet potato, peeled and diced
4 quality gluten-free wraps or thin pizza bases
80 g (2¾ oz) Garlic & chive cashew cream 'cheese' (page 130)

TOMATO PASTE
300 g (10½ oz/2 cups) semi-dried or sundried tomatoes
3 tablespoons water
1 garlic clove, peeled
1 teaspoon coconut sugar
1 teaspoon dried oregano

TOPPINGS
½ red onion, finely diced
65 g (2¼ oz/½ cup) olives, pitted and sliced
70 g (2½ oz/½ cup) red capsicum (bell pepper), finely diced
45 g (1½ oz/½ cup) mushrooms, diced
35 g (1¼ oz/½ cup) curly leaf kale, stalks removed, chopped
20 g (¾ oz/½ cup) fresh basil leaves, roughly chopped

Preheat the oven to 180°C (360°F) fan-forced.

For the base, using a steaming basket, steam the sweet potato until it is soft right through. Place in a bowl and mash until smooth.

Spread two wraps with the garlic and chive cashew cream 'cheese', followed by all of the mashed sweet potato, before gently laying another wrap over the top of each and pressing down gently, especially around the edges.

Place all the tomato paste ingredients in a blender or food processor. Pulse to combine, then blend until evenly mixed. Spread this mixture over the top of the layered wraps.

Sprinkle with the onion, olives and red capsicum and bake for 10 minutes. Remove from the oven and add the mushrooms, kale and basil. Return to the oven and bake for a further 10 minutes. Slice and serve.

BAKED SWEET SPUDS

When you think of baked potatoes it often conjures up images of steaming potatoes doused in bolognese sauce and copious amounts of melted cheese. Not in this case. There is nothing quite like the comfort of a baked potato. The fillings in this baked spud are tasty, nourishing and satisfying. Just the way it should be.

Serves 2
Prep time: 10 minutes
Cook time: 50 minutes

BAKED POTATO
4 small sweet potatoes

FILLINGS
250 g (9 oz/1 cup) Garlic tahini dressing (page 132)
100 g (3½ oz/1 cup) red cabbage, finely shredded
50 g (1¾ oz/½ cup) spring onion (scallion), thinly sliced
1 avocado, peeled, stone removed, sliced

TO SERVE
30 g (1 oz/1 cup) flat-leaf (Italian) parsley
80 g (2¾ oz) Garlic & chive cashew cream 'cheese' (optional, page 130)

Preheat the oven to 200°C (390°F) fan-forced.

Wash the sweet potatoes and score them lengthways three-quarters of the way through. Place on a baking tray, scored side up, and bake for 50 minutes.

Once cooked through, remove the potatoes from the oven and, using two spoons, gently push the sides apart to create a big enough gap to add the fillings.

Begin filling by pouring the tahini dressing into each sweet potato. Follow with the red cabbage, spring onion and avocado, finishing with a sprinkling of parsley and a dollop of garlic and chive cashew cream 'cheese' (or serve it on the side), if desired.

GREEN MUSHIE
NOODLE BOWL

Discovering that you can make noodles out of whole vegetables has definitely been a highlight of my journey into wholefoods. Growing up, one of my favourite meals was spaghetti with parsley pesto. I wanted to create something reminiscent of this without the refined wheat or dairy, and I couldn't resist throwing in a bit of extra nutrition by adding mushrooms.

Serves 2
Prep time: 10 minutes
Cook time: 10 minutes

1 tablespoon plant-based oil

540 g (1 lb 3 oz/6 cups) button mushrooms, sliced

2 garlic cloves, peeled and crushed

1 tablespoon fresh thyme leaves

30 g (1 oz/1 cup) parsley, finely chopped

2 large zucchini (courgettes), spiralised

⅛ teaspoon quality mineral salt

TO SERVE

70 g (2½ oz/½ cup) pine nuts

15 g (½ oz/½ cup) parsley (optional)

60 g (2 oz/½ cup) Cashew 'parmesan' (page 130)

Heat the oil in a large non-stick frying pan. Add the mushrooms, garlic and thyme and sauté over medium heat for about 10 minutes, or until cooked through. Reduce to low heat, add the parsley, zucchini noodles and salt and stir through.

Transfer to a large serving bowl and top with the pine nuts and parsley leaves, if desired. Add the cashew 'parmesan' to taste.

RAW SATAY PAD THAI SALAD

This is such a perfect dish to take along to any summer gathering. In this recipe I have used zucchini noodles made with a spiraliser. Spiralisers are wonderful, inexpensive pieces of equipment that can turn many raw vegetables into crisp noodles to use in any number of salads. In this recipe I chose to leave the skins on the zucchini as they contain good nutrients. However, if you are after a more traditional noodle, simply peel the zucchini before spiralising. If you do not have a spiraliser you can also slice zucchini into flat ribbon noodles with a peeler.

Serves 2
Prep time: 10 minutes

SALAD

2 medium zucchini (courgettes),
   spiralised
200 g (7 oz/2 cups) red cabbage, finely
   shredded
100 g (3½ oz/1 cup) pea shoots
40 g (1½ oz/½ cup) spring onions
   (scallions), finely chopped
1 medium carrot, sliced into ribbons
½ large red capsicum (bell pepper),
   thinly sliced
30 g (1 oz/1 cup) fresh coriander
   (cilantro) leaves

DRESSING

250 g (9 oz/1 cup) Satay sauce (page 128)

TO SERVE

70 g (2½ oz/½ cup) cashew nuts
1 tablespoon coriander (cilantro) leaves
   (optional)

Combine all the salad ingredients in a bowl and toss together. Add the satay sauce and mix well (or serve it on the side if you prefer). Top with the cashew nuts and extra coriander to serve, if desired.

MEXICAN CHILLI
FRIES & GUACAMOLE

Easy to make and unbelievably yummy, these sweet potato fries can be served with a variety of dishes to add a tasty and filling element. I love serving them with the Mushie burgers with the lot (page 72). They are also great as a snack dipped into delicious spicy guacamole.

Serves 2
Prep time: 20 minutes
Cook time: 30 minutes

CHILLI FRIES

1 kg (2 lb 3 oz) sweet potato, washed and cut into 1–2 cm (½–¾ in) wide fries

1 tablespoon sunflower oil

120 g (4½ oz/1 cup) Cashew 'parmesan' (page 130)

¼ teaspoon chilli powder (more if you like it spicy)

1 teaspoon ground cumin

1 teaspoon paprika

2 teaspoons coconut sugar

GUACAMOLE

2 large avocados, peeled and stones removed

1 mild red chilli, thinly sliced (seeds removed, if desired)

5 g (¼ oz/¼ cup) coriander (cilantro) leaves

1 tablespoon thinly sliced fresh chives

2 teaspoons apple-cider vinegar

1 lime

1 pinch quality mineral salt

1 teaspoon smoked paprika

Preheat the oven to 200°C (390°F) fan-forced.

Toss the fries in the sunflower oil and spread on a baking tray lined with baking paper. Bake for 30 minutes. Turn the fries and cook for a further 10 minutes.

Remove the fries from the oven and allow to cool for 10 minutes.

Mix the cashew 'parmesan', chilli powder, ground cumin, paprika and coconut sugar together and sprinkle over the fries.

For the guacamole, mash the avocados, then add the sliced chilli, coriander, chives, apple-cider vinegar and a squeeze of lime and mix well. Sprinkle with the smoked paprika and serve.

MUSHIE BURGERS
WITH THE LOT

Flavourful yet simple and super healthy, these burgers are a wonderful option for those following a gluten-free diet. Using two large mushrooms is an ingenious swap for a traditional bread bun as they offer so much nutrition and satisfaction and, in my opinion, are much tastier.

Makes 4 burgers
Prep time: 30 minutes
Cook time: 30 minutes

PATTIES

1 large (400 g/14 oz) sweet potato, peeled and diced

250 g (9 oz) tinned cannellini beans, drained and rinsed

30 g (1 oz/1 cup) flat-leaf (Italian) parsley, chopped

40 g (1½ oz/½ cup) spring onion (scallion), thinly sliced

¼ teaspoon quality mineral salt

1 garlic clove, finely chopped or crushed

1 tablespoon fresh thyme leaves

35 g (1¼ oz/¼ cup) sesame seeds

'BUNS'

8 large portobello mushrooms, stalks removed

1 teaspoon sunflower oil

FILLINGS

2 cos (romaine) lettuce leaves, halved

1 lime, halved

1 large avocado, peeled, stone removed, roughly mashed

4 tablespoons Beetroot & dill relish (page 122)

20 g (¾ oz/¼ cup) bean shoots

Preheat the oven to 180°C (360°F) fan-forced.

Steam the sweet potato in a steaming basket for about 10 minutes until you can easily pierce it with a fork. Transfer to a bowl. Add the cannellini beans, parsley, spring onion, salt, garlic and thyme and mash together with a fork, mixing well.

Mould the mixture into four patties. Roll the patties in the sesame seeds and place them on a baking paper-lined baking tray. Bake for 30 minutes, turning halfway through the cooking time.

For the 'buns', brush the top of each mushroom with a little oil, then heat a non-stick frying pan and toast the mushrooms on both sides.

To assemble your burgers, place half the mushrooms, top side down, on four plates, then simply stack with a few pieces of cos lettuce and one patty each. Squeeze lime juice over the avocado and spread over the patties. Top with beetroot relish and a sprinkling of bean shoots.

Place the remaining mushrooms on top to complete the burger. Serve.

GINGER & MISO GLAZED EGGPLANT

Japanese food is one of my all-time favourite cuisines. I am forever taking the Japanese dishes I enjoy most and reconstructing them with fresh, readily available ingredients, and this recipe is no exception. The contrast of the gooey, soft, sweet and sour eggplant and the fresh, crunchy salad is just delicious.

Serves 2
Prep time: 15 minutes
Cook time: 10 minutes

EGGPLANT

2 medium eggplants (aubergines)

quality mineral salt

3 tablespoons miso paste

3 tablespoons coconut sugar

2 tablespoons apple-cider vinegar, plus extra for the salad

3 teaspoons grated fresh ginger

SALAD

200 g (7 oz/2 cups) red cabbage, shredded

2 medium carrots, sliced into ribbons

1 medium avocado, peeled, stone removed, diced

100 g (3½ oz/1 cup) mung bean sprouts

TO SERVE

1 tablespoon thinly sliced spring onion (scallion)

2 teaspoons sesame seeds

Preheat the oven to 200°C (390°F) fan-forced.

Begin by slicing the eggplants in half and scoring the flesh in a diamond pattern, being careful not to pierce the skin.

Place the eggplant, skin side down, on a baking tray lined with baking paper and sprinkle with salt. Bake for 20 minutes. The eggplant should be soft to the touch.

Mix together the miso paste, coconut sugar, apple-cider vinegar and ginger in a bowl. Spread two-thirds of the mixture over the eggplant and return to the oven for 15 minutes, or until the glaze begins to caramelise.

Toss the salad ingredients together, add another splash of apple-cider vinegar to the remaining glaze mixture and stir together. Pour this over the salad.

Sprinkle the eggplant with the spring onion and sesame seeds and serve with a generous helping of salad.

BAKED FALAFEL WRAPS

A fun, colourful twist on a classic falafel wrap, this is a light and delicious combination. The cabbage leaf makes a great crunchy alternative to a wheat wrap. Use whatever salad ingredients you have on hand to fill the wrap. Here I have used a deconstructed tabbouleh. The falafel balls are simple to make and are a delicious addition to a lunchtime salad the following day.

Makes about 6 wraps
Prep time: 20 minutes
Cook time: 30 minutes

FALAFEL
500 g (1 lb 2 oz) tinned chickpeas, drained and rinsed
½ large onion, diced
30 g (1 oz/1 cup) flat-leaf (Italian) parsley
1 tablespoon ground cumin
1 tablespoon freshly squeezed lemon juice
½ teaspoon quality mineral salt
2 tablespoons white sesame seeds
2 tablespoons black sesame seeds

WRAPS
6 large red cabbage leaves
100 g (3½ oz/1 cup) cherry tomatoes, quartered
30 g (1 oz/1 cup) flat-leaf (Italian) parsley
40 g (1½ oz/1 cup) alfalfa sprouts

TO SERVE
255 g (9 oz/1 cup) Mint tahini dressing (page 132)
5 g (¼ oz/¼ cup) fresh mint leaves (optional)

Preheat the oven to 180°C (360°F) fan-forced.

Place all the falafel ingredients, except the sesame seeds, in a food processor. Pulse to combine, then blend until smooth.

Line a large baking tray with baking paper. Roll the mixture into balls roughly 3 cm (1¼ in) in diameter, then roll the falafel balls in the sesame seeds before placing them on the tray. Bake for around 30 minutes, or until lightly browned.

To assemble the wraps, layer the fillings inside the cabbage leaves and top with the baked falafel. Drizzle with mint tahini dressing and a few mint leaves, if desired.

ROASTED ROOT VEGETABLE
PESTO SALAD

Once you have experienced this salad, don't be surprised if you begin to crave it. Traditional pesto is often made with parmesan cheese, but this mix of pine nuts, nutritional yeast, basil, olive oil, garlic and salt gives it the same scrumptious flavour without the processed dairy. I always make a double batch when taking it to a gathering. There is never any left.

Serves 4
Prep time: 30 minutes
Cook time: 35 minutes

SALAD
80 g (2¾ oz/½ cup) almonds

1 large beetroot (beet), peeled and diced

1 large zucchini (courgette), diced

1 medium eggplant (aubergine), diced

1 medium sweet potato, diced

45 g (1½ oz/1½ cups) rocket (arugula)

45 g (1½ oz/1½ cups) baby English
  spinach

2 ripe tomatoes, diced

1 large avocado, peeled, stone removed,
  diced

125 g (4 oz/1 cup) black olives, pitted

PESTO
140 g (5 oz/1 cup) raw cashew nuts

70 g (2½ oz/½ cup) pine nuts

60 g (2 oz/1½ cups) fresh basil leaves

20 g (¾ oz/¼ cup) nutritional yeast

2 garlic cloves, peeled

1 tablespoon cold-pressed olive oil

½ teaspoon quality mineral salt

TO SERVE
juice of 1 lemon

Preheat the oven to 200°C (390°F) fan-forced.

Heat a non-stick frying pan and lightly toast the almonds. Set aside to cool.

Spread the beetroot, zucchini, eggplant and sweet potato on baking paper-lined baking trays and bake for 30 minutes.

Meanwhile, combine all the pesto ingredients in a food processor and pulse eight to ten times until evenly combined. The mixture will remain quite chunky.

Lightly crush the cooled almonds.

Once the vegetables are cooked through, remove them from the oven and leave to cool. Then layer the rocket, spinach, tomato, roast vegetables, avocado, olives and almonds in a large mixing bowl.

Dollop the pesto over the salad and squeeze lemon juice over it all. Toss to combine, then serve.

BEETROOT & DILL RICE PAPER ROLLS

These tasty, fresh little pockets are a quick and easy meal when I don't know what to make. They never disappoint. There are endless combinations of delicious wholefoods to roll up into rice paper, and these are my favourites. The satay dipping sauce is the perfect addition to these colourful crowd-pleasers.

Makes about 15 small rice paper rolls
Prep time: 30 minutes

RICE PAPER ROLLS

½ lime

1 large avocado, peeled, stone removed, thinly sliced

15–20 rice paper sheets

165 g (6 oz/¾ cup) Beetroot & dill relish (page 122)

½ red capsicum (bell pepper), sliced lengthways

20 g (¾ oz/1 cup) fresh dill, stalks removed

1 tablespoon sesame seeds

80 g (2¾ oz/2 cups) alfalfa sprouts

TO SERVE

5 g (¼ oz/⅓ cup) fresh dill (optional)

250 g (9 oz/1 cup) Satay sauce (page 128)

Squeeze the lime over the sliced avocado. Set aside.

Carefully fill a large bowl with hot water, wide enough to lie the rice paper in. Slide a rice paper sheet into the water and gently press down until fully submerged. Wait 1–2 minutes until the rice paper is translucent and soft. Gently remove it from the water and spread it out on a clean chopping board.

Immediately slide another rice paper sheet in to soften while you fill your ready rice paper sheet. Repeat this process as you construct your rice paper rolls.

To fill the rice paper rolls, stack a small amount of each ingredient about 3 cm (1¼ in) from the edge, finishing with the alfalfa sprouts.

To roll, pick up the edge closest to you, folding over the filling while simultaneously pushing down on the fillings, and roll over once. Fold the right and left edges in as far as they will go and continue rolling. Spread the finished rolls out on a plate to cool.

Once you are finished, using a hot, sharp, wet knife, slice each roll in half crossways. Scatter with fresh dill, if desired, and serve with a small bowl of satay sauce for dipping.

DESSERTS

RAW BLISS BITES
3 WAYS

These are the perfect energy snacks to take with you on the go. Jam-packed with nutrition, they can be ready in less than 10 minutes and will keep in an airtight container in the refrigerator for up to a week. I love experimenting with different ingredients for fillings and delicious coatings. There are endless options as far as nuts, seeds and powders go. These are my three go-to flavours that are always on high rotation at our house.

RAINBOW ENERGY

Makes about 20 × 3 cm (1¼ in) balls
Prep time: 10 minutes

80 g (2¾ oz/½ cup) activated buckwheat

65 g (2¼ oz/½ cup) pistachio nuts

60 g (2 oz/½ cup) goji berries

20 g (¾ oz/½ cup) coconut flakes

½ teaspoon vanilla powder

15 medjool dates, pitted

Combine the buckwheat, pistachio nuts, goji berries, coconut flakes and vanilla powder in a food processor. Turn to high speed and, keeping the motor running, add the dates, one at a time. Continue to process for a further 1–2 minutes, or until sticky. Roll into balls and store in an airtight jar or container in the refrigerator.

AFTER-DINNER MINT

Makes about 20 × 3 cm (1¼ in) balls
Prep time: 10 minutes

240 g (8½ oz/1½ cups) raw almonds

10 medjool dates, pitted

35 g (1¼ oz/¼ cup) cacao powder

2 tablespoons cacao nibs

5 drops organic food-grade peppermint essential oil

⅛ teaspoon quality mineral salt

15 g (½ oz/¼ cup) desiccated (shredded) coconut

In a food processor, blitz the almonds for 5 seconds. Keeping the motor running, add the dates one at a time. Add all the other ingredients, except the coconut, and continue to process until evenly combined. Roll into balls, then coat with the desiccated coconut. Store in an airtight container in the refrigerator.

CHOC PEANUT
BUTTER

Makes about 20 × 3 cm (1¼ in) balls
Prep time: 10 minutes

160 g (5½ oz/1 cup) raw almonds

10 medjool dates, pitted

2 tablespoons natural peanut butter

½ teaspoon quality mineral salt

2 tablespoons cacao nibs

In a food processor, blitz the almonds for 5 seconds. Keeping the motor running, add the dates, one at a time. Stop processing and add the peanut butter and salt. Blend for a further 8–10 seconds. Add the cacao nibs and pulse the mixture until the nibs are evenly combined but not entirely broken up. Roll into balls and store in the refrigerator.

LIME & BLACKBERRY LAYER CAKE

Nature holds the finest colour palette, if you ask me. There is absolutely no need for artificial colours or flavours, and this slice is proof. It is as vibrant in flavour as it is in colour, and is guaranteed to get the tick of approval.

Serves 12 (small pieces)
Prep time: 40 minutes (+ 14 hours soaking and setting)

BASE
240 g (8½ oz/1½ cups) raw almonds
10 medjool dates, pitted
1 tablespoon frozen raspberries, crushed

LIME LAYER
1 large avocado, peeled and stone
   removed
60 ml (2 fl oz/¼ cup) freshly squeezed
   lime juice
125 ml (4 fl oz/½ cup) melted coconut oil
80 ml (2½ fl oz/⅓ cup) maple syrup

BLACKBERRY LAYER
210 g (7½ oz/1½ cups) cashew nuts,
   soaked for 8 hours, drained and rinsed
125 ml (4 fl oz/½ cup) melted coconut oil
90 g (3 oz/⅔ cup) blackberries, fresh or
   thawed from frozen
80 ml (2½ fl oz/⅓ cup) maple syrup
60 ml (2 fl oz/¼ cup) freshly squeezed
   lime juice
1 teaspoon vanilla powder
1 pinch quality mineral salt

TOPPINGS
¼ cup edible dried flowers (optional)
30 g (1 oz/¼ cup) pistachio nuts, crushed
extra berries (optional)

Line a 15 × 25 cm (6 × 10 in) slice tin with baking paper.

For the base, blitz the almonds in a food processor for 5 seconds. Keeping the motor running, add the dates, one at a time. Once well combined and slightly sticky, press the mixture into the base of the slice tin. Sprinkle with the raspberries and gently press into the base mixture. Place in the freezer while you make the lime layer.

In a food processor, combine all the lime layer ingredients on high until very smooth and creamy. You may need to pause the processor to push the mixture down the sides as you go. Pour the mixture on top of the base and spread gently and evenly with a spatula. Return to the freezer for 2 hours to set.

Once set, make the blackberry layer. Process all the blackberry layer ingredients on high speed until smooth and creamy. Spread the mixture over the lime layer and sprinkle with dried edible flowers, crushed pistachio nuts or extra berries, if desired. Return to the freezer for at least 4 hours to set.

Remove the slice from the freezer about 10–15 minutes before slicing and serving.

FRED & GINGER
SURPRISE CAKES

These little surprises are bursting with hidden goodness. Not only do they taste amazing but the ginger and lemon also aid digestion, boost immunity and settle the stomach — not a bad way to get some extra goodness into your diet.

Makes 24 mini surprise cakes
Prep time: 30 minutes (+ 12½ hours soaking and setting)

BASE
240 g (8½ oz/1½ cups) raw almonds
10 medjool dates, pitted
70 g (2½ oz/½ cup) frozen raspberries, crushed

GINGER LEMON FILLING
280 g (10 oz/2 cups) cashew nuts, soaked for 8 hours, drained and rinsed
125 ml (4 fl oz/½ cup) freshly squeezed lemon juice
125 ml (4 fl oz/½ cup) maple syrup
125 ml (4 fl oz/½ cup) melted coconut oil
1 tablespoon finely grated fresh ginger
½ teaspoon vanilla powder
1 pinch quality mineral salt

CHOCOLATE COCONUT COATING
1 batch Raw chocolate (page 117)
45 g (1½ oz/½ cup) desiccated (shredded) coconut

YOU WILL ALSO NEED
2 trays mini silicone cupcake moulds (with 12 × 5 cm/2 in diameter holes)
24 popsicle sticks

Make the base mixture by adding the almonds to a food processor and blending on high speed for 5 seconds. With the motor still running, add the pitted dates, one at a time.

Divide this mixture between the silicone cupcake moulds and gently press into the base of the holes. Scatter with the crushed raspberries and place in the freezer while you make the ginger lemon filling.

Add all the ginger and lemon filling ingredients to a blender. Pulse to combine, then blend until smooth and creamy. Pour the ginger and lemon mixture over the bases and carefully push a popsicle stick into each one, making sure that it stands vertically.

Return to the freezer for 4 hours to set.

Once set, melt the raw chocolate. Line a tray with baking paper, ready to place the chocolate-dipped cakes onto. Carefully remove each cake from the mould and, holding it by the popsicle stick and on an angle, dip it into the chocolate. Remove and roll in the desiccated coconut. Place top-down on a baking paper-lined tray and repeat for all of the mini cakes. Return to the freezer for a further 30 minutes to set.

Remove from the freezer 20 minutes before serving.

Oh hey there
good lookin'

X Natural Harry

JAFFA MOUSSE TART

Chocolate and orange is one of those sweet combinations that I can't get enough of. This cake is so rich and creamy, it is hard to believe it has no dairy, eggs or anything artificial. I like to sprinkle some grated orange zest over it just before serving. Not only does it add a beautiful colour, but the orange zest is what holds that fresh scent from the orange oil.

Serves about 12
Prep time: 30 minutes (+ 16 hours soaking and setting)

BASE
240 g (8½ oz/1½ cups) raw almonds
10 medjool dates, pitted

CHOCOLATE ORANGE FILLING
280 g (10 oz/2 cups) cashew nuts,
   soaked for 8 hours, drained and rinsed
125 ml (4 fl oz/½ cup) almond milk
125 ml (4 fl oz/½ cup) maple syrup
125 ml (4 fl oz/½ cup) melted coconut oil
70 g (2½ oz/½ cup) cacao powder
1 teaspoon vanilla powder
7 drops organic food-grade orange
   essential oil
1 pinch quality mineral salt

TOPPING
1 tablespoon finely grated orange zest
1 tablespoon cacao nibs
2 tablespoons orange tea or dried edible
   flowers (optional)

Line an 18 cm (7 in) round springform cake tin with baking paper.

For the base, blend the almonds on high speed in a food processor. Keeping the motor running, add the dates, one at a time. Continue to process until sticky.

Press the base mixture into the bottom of the cake tin, cover and place in the freezer while you make the filling.

For the chocolate orange filling, combine all the ingredients in a blender or food processor. Pulse to combine, then blend on high speed until smooth and creamy. Pour over the cake base and smooth with a spatula.

Sprinkle with grated orange zest, cacao nibs and orange tea or dried edible flowers, if desired. Return to the freezer for 4 hours to set. Place in the refrigerator for 4 hours to thaw before serving.

NUT-FREE
CARAMEL SLICE

This delicious, sweet-as-pie slice may not win any prizes for looks, but it sure is scrumptious. Packed full of fibre and antioxidants, the crunchy base and gooey caramel make for a lovely contrast.

Makes 18 small squares
Prep time: 30 minutes (+ 4½ hours setting)

BASE
240 g (8½ oz/1½ cups) plain activated buckwheat
15 medjool dates, pitted

CARAMEL LAYER
30 medjool dates, pitted
60 ml (2 fl oz/¼ cup) warm water
2 tablespoons coconut oil
1 teaspoon vanilla powder
⅛ teaspoon quality mineral salt

CHOCOLATE TOPPING
100 g (3½ oz) cacao butter, finely chopped or grated
80 ml (2½ fl oz/⅓ cup) coconut oil
70 g (2½ oz/½ cup) cacao powder
60 ml (2 fl oz/¼ cup) maple syrup

Line the bottom of a 15 × 25 cm (6 × 10 in) brownie or slice tin with baking paper.

Combine the base ingredients in a food processor. Blitz until the buckwheat and dates are evenly combined and sticking together when pressed. Gently press the mixture into the base of the tin and place in the freezer while you make the caramel layer.

Combine all the caramel layer ingredients in a food processor. Pulse to combine, then blend until super smooth and creamy. You may have to stop the motor every now and then to push the mixture down the sides to ensure it combines evenly. Once the caramel layer mixture is ready, remove the tin from the freezer and pour the caramel mixture on top of the base, smoothing it all the way to the edges with a spatula.

Return the tin to the freezer for about 4 hours.

To make the chocolate topping, melt the cacao butter in a double boiler. Once completely melted, add the coconut oil, cacao powder and maple syrup, and whisk them in well.

Pour the chocolate topping over the caramel layer and return the slice to the freezer for 30 minutes.

Remove 10 minutes before slicing to allow the chocolate topping to thaw a little. Slice with a sharp, hot knife.

PASSION & LEMON 'LOVE CAKE'

This cake was created as a custom order and it looked so pretty and tasted so delicious I just had to make it again, and again, and again. The fruits available in summer really lend themselves to delicious creamy cheesecakes made with plant-based wholefoods — and passionfruit is no exception.

Serves 12 (or more)
Prep time: 40 minutes (+ 14 hours soaking and setting)

BASE

240 g (8½ oz/1½ cups) raw almonds
15 g (½ oz/¼ cup) desiccated (shredded)
  coconut
10 medjool dates, pitted

PASSIONFRUIT LAYER

125 g (4½ oz/½ cup) fresh passionfruit
  pulp
280 g (10 oz/2 cups) cashew nuts, soaked
  for 8 hours, drained and rinsed
60 ml (2 fl oz/¼ cup) freshly squeezed
  lemon juice
125 ml (4 fl oz/½ cup) maple syrup
1 pinch quality mineral salt
125 ml (4 fl oz/½ cup) melted coconut oil

LEMON LAYER

280 g (10 oz/2 cups) cashew nuts, soaked
  for 8 hours, drained and rinsed
60 ml (2 fl oz/¼ cup) freshly squeezed
  lemon juice
125 ml (4 fl oz/½ cup) maple syrup
1 pinch quality mineral salt
125 ml (4 fl oz/½ cup) melted coconut oil
½ teaspoon vanilla powder

TOPPINGS

70 g (2½ oz/½ cup) fresh or frozen
  raspberries
1 tablespoon edible fresh or dried flowers

Line an 18 cm (7 in) round springform cake tin with baking paper.

For the base, blend the almonds and coconut in a food processor on high speed for 5 seconds. Then, keeping the motor running, add the dates, one at a time. Check that the mixture is sticking together. Continue to process until it stays together when pressed. Gently press into the bottom of the cake tin, cover and place in the freezer.

Place all the passionfruit layer ingredients in a food processor or blender. Begin to process on low speed and slowly increase the speed. Blend until smooth and creamy. You will still be able to see specks of passionfruit seed in the mixture. Carefully pour the mixture over the cake base and spread evenly all the way to the sides using a spatula. Cover again and return to the freezer for about 2 hours to set.

Once the passionfruit layer is set, combine all the lemon layer ingredients in the food processor and repeat the same process as for the passionfruit layer. Remove the cake from the freezer and spread evenly with the lemon layer. Sprinkle with raspberries and edible flowers and return to the freezer for a minimum of 4 hours to set.

Before serving, allow to thaw in the refrigerator for 3—4 hours.

PEPPERMINT CRISP SLICE

This old favourite is one of the original slice recipes I made when we first opened the little caravan and I still make it regularly to this day. You just cannot beat the combination of fresh, bitey mint and creamy dark chocolate. It really is a match made in heaven.

Serves 12 (or more)
Prep time: 45 minutes (+ 16 hours soaking and setting)

BASE
240 g (8½ oz/1½ cups) raw almonds
10–15 medjool dates, pitted
35 g (1¼ oz/¼ cup) cacao powder

MINT CREAM LAYER
90 g (3 oz/1 cup) desiccated (shredded) coconut
140 g (5 oz/1 cup) cashew nuts, soaked for 8 hours, drained and rinsed
125 ml (4 fl oz/½ cup) melted coconut oil
125 ml (4 fl oz/½ cup) maple syrup
4 drops organic food-grade peppermint oil
½ teaspoon vanilla powder
1 pinch of salt

CHOCOLATE LAYER
125 ml (4 fl oz/½ cup) melted coconut oil
105 g (3½ oz/¾ cup) cashew nuts, soaked for 8 hours, drained and rinsed
70 g (2½ oz/½ cup) cacao powder
60 ml (2 fl oz/¼ cup) maple syrup
½ teaspoon vanilla powder

TO SERVE
fresh mint leaves (optional)

Line the bottom of a 15 × 25 cm (6 x 10 in) brownie or slice tin with baking paper.

Combine the base ingredients in a food processor, then blitz until it's a breadcrumb-like consistency and it starts to stick together. Gently press the mixture into the base of the tin and place in the freezer while you make the mint cream layer.

For the mint cream layer, blend the desiccated coconut on high speed until smooth. Add all the other mint cream ingredients and blend until smooth. Pour over the base, spreading evenly with a spatula. Place in the freezer for a minimum of 4 hours to set.

Combine all the chocolate layer ingredients in the food processor, pulse to combine, then blend until smooth. Gently spread the chocolate layer over the slice, then return to the freezer for 1–2 hours to set.

Remove from the freezer 10 minutes before serving. Slice with a sharp, hot knife. Garnish with mint leaves, if desired.

TURKISH DELIGHT CREAM POPS

These are a real treat. They may take a little while to make but it is well worth it. They are simply delicious. The creamy centre with pockets of fresh raspberry along with the thin chocolate shell is divine. I love to dress mine up and make them extra special by rolling them in crushed pistachio nuts and rose petals. These are perfect for any special occasion. Bonus points for being super healthy.

Makes 16 × 100 ml (3½ fl oz) cream pops
Prep time: 40 minutes (+ 16 hours soaking and setting)

FILLING
560 g (1 lb 4 oz/4 cups) cashew nuts,
    soaked for 8 hours, drained and rinsed
250 ml (8½ fl oz/1 cup) freshly squeezed
    lemon juice
250 ml (8½ fl oz/1 cup) maple syrup
1 tablespoon organic food-grade
    rosewater
½ teaspoon vanilla powder
⅛ teaspoon quality mineral salt
210 g (7½ oz/1½ cups) frozen raspberries

CHOCOLATE PISTACHIO COATING
1 tablespoon pistachio nuts
1 tablespoon crushed organic, unsprayed,
    edible rose petals
1 batch Raw chocolate (page 117)

YOU WILL ALSO NEED
16 × 100 ml (3½ fl oz) (or equivalent)
    popsicle moulds
16 × popsicle sticks

Combine all the filling ingredients, except the raspberries, in a food processor or blender. Pulse to combine, then process on high speed until smooth and creamy.

Spoon half the mixture into the bottom of the popsicle moulds, then sprinkle the raspberries into each mould on top of the mixture. Spoon the remaining mixture into the moulds to fill. Place a popsicle stick in each mould and gently stir the filling so that the raspberries are spread throughout and no air gaps remain. Leave a popsicle stick in each mould and transfer the moulds to the freezer for 8 hours or overnight to set.

For the coating, lightly crush the pistachio nuts by pulsing them in a food processor. Add the rose petals and mix together.

Melt the raw chocolate and pour it into a tall, wide jar or container. Remove the popsicles from the moulds. Dip each one into the raw chocolate, then gently roll one side in the pistachio and rose petal mixture. Place on a baking paper-lined tray and return to the freezer for 20 minutes to set.

Store in the freezer and remove 10 minutes before eating.

PINK ROSE LEMONADE
'CHEESECAKES'

These mini delights taste as pretty as they look and are perfect with a cup of herbal tea in the afternoon sunshine. The rosewater and the tang of lemon makes them refreshing, creamy and fragrant.

Makes 24 baby 'cheesecakes'
Prep time: 30 minutes (+ 12 hours soaking and setting)

BASE
240 g (8½ oz/1½ cups) raw almonds
10 medjool dates, pitted

LEMON LAYER
140 g (5 oz/1 cup) cashew nuts, soaked for
   8 hours, drained and rinsed
60 ml (2 fl oz/¼ cup) freshly squeezed
   lemon juice
60 ml (2 fl oz/¼ cup) maple syrup
60 ml (2 fl oz/¼ cup) melted coconut oil
⅛ teaspoon vanilla powder
1 pinch quality mineral salt

ROSE LAYER
140 g (5 oz/1 cup) cashew nuts, soaked for
   8 hours, drained and rinsed
60 ml (2 fl oz/¼ cup) freshly squeezed
   lemon juice
60 ml (2 fl oz/¼ cup) maple syrup
60 ml (2 fl oz/¼ cup) melted coconut oil
1 tablespoon raspberries, fresh or thawed
   from frozen
2 teaspoons organic food-grade rosewater
⅛ teaspoon vanilla powder
1 pinch quality salt

TOPPINGS
2 tablespoons coconut flakes
1 tablespoon dried rose petals (optional)
1 tablespoon grated lemon zest

To make the base, blend the almonds in a food processor on high speed for about 5 deseconds. With the motor still running, add the dates, one at a time, until a sticky dough forms.

Divide the mixture between two silicone trays with 12 × 5 cm (2½ in) diameter holes, and press into the base of the holes. Place the trays in the freezer while you make the lemon layer.

For the lemon layer, add all the ingredients to a blender or food processor. Pulse to combine, then blend until smooth. Spoon the mixture onto the bases in the moulds, then return to the freezer for 2 hours to set.

Once the lemon layer is set, combine all the rose layer ingredients in a blender. Pulse to combine, then blend until super smooth. Spoon the mixture on top of the lemon layer in the moulds and gently push into the sides to make sure there are no gaps.

Sprinkle with the coconut flakes, lemon zest and rose petals, if desired, and return to the freezer for 2 hours to set.

Remove from the moulds and place in the refrigerator for 1 hour before serving.

CARAVAN WHEELS

A wholefood take on that giant chocolate-coated, jam-filled old favourite, just minus all the preservatives, refined grains and sugar. These wheels are a delicious balance of dark chocolate, creamy marshmallow, tangy jam and sweet, chewy cookie – and I warn you that they are moreish too!

Makes 25—30 wheels
Prep time: 50 minutes (+ 14½ hours soaking and setting)

MARSHMALLOW

180 g (6½ oz/2 cups) desiccated
(shredded) coconut
280 g (10 oz/2 cups) cashew nuts, soaked
for 8 hours, drained and rinsed
125 ml (4 fl oz/½ cup) maple syrup
1 teaspoon vanilla
1 pinch quality mineral salt

COOKIES

480 g (1 lb 1 oz/3 cups) raw almonds
20 medjool dates, pitted

CHIA JAM

300 g (10½ oz/1 cup) Maqui berry & lime
chia jam (page 142)

CHOCOLATE COATING

1 batch Raw chocolate (page 117)

For the marshmallow, blend the coconut on high speed in a food processor until a smooth thick liquid forms. Place the cashew nuts on top of the coconut in the processor. Add all the other marshmallow ingredients and blend until smooth. Pour into a bowl, cover and place in the refrigerator to set.

Make the cookie mixture in two batches. Add half the almonds to a food processor and blitz on high speed. With the motor still running, add 10 of the pitted dates, one at a time, blending until the mixture begins to stick together. Place the mixture in a bowl and repeat this process with the other half of the ingredients. Then combine all the cookie mixture in one bowl.

Form the mixture into a large ball, then roll out onto baking paper with a rolling pin. Use a 5 cm (2½ in) cookie cutter to cut the mixture into cookies. Spread the cookies out on a baking paper-lined tray as you go. Place in the freezer to set for about 2 hours.

Once set, spread half the cookies with a generous dollop of marshmallow and create a well in the centre for the chia jam. Place another cookie on top of each and return to the freezer for a minimum of 4 hours to set.

Melt the raw chocolate in a small basin. Dip each frozen cookie in the chocolate and return to the paper-lined tray. Drizzle with extra chocolate and return to the freezer for 20 minutes.

Remove from the freezer 20 minutes before serving.

COOKIE DOUGH & CREAM SLICE

Every time I enjoy a slice of this delicious creation I am amazed at the creamy texture and the subtle contrast in flavours. I add berries to many a raw dessert recipe, as I feel they always give it that little lift. In this recipe the raspberries make the perfect contrast to the creamy filling and delicious chunks of raw cookie dough.

Serves 12 (or more)
Prep time: 30 minutes (+ 12 hours soaking and setting)

BASE
240 g (8½ oz/1½ cups) raw almonds
35 g (1¼ oz/¼ cup) cacao powder
10 medjool dates, pitted

COOKIE DOUGH
80 g (2¾ oz/½ cup) almonds
1 tablespoon cacao powder
6–8 medjool dates, pitted

CREAM FILLING
280 g (10 oz/2 cups) cashew nuts, soaked
   for 8 hours, drained and rinsed
125 ml (4 fl oz/½ cup) maple syrup
125 ml (4 fl oz/½ cup) almond milk
1 teaspoon vanilla powder
1 pinch salt
125 ml (4 fl oz/½ cup) melted coconut oil

TOPPINGS
70 g (2½ oz/½ cup) frozen raspberries,
   crushed
50 g (1¾ oz/¼ cup) cacao nibs

Line a 15 × 25 cm (6 × 10 in) slice tin with baking paper.

Make the base by blending the almonds and cacao powder in a food processor on high speed for 5 seconds. Keeping the motor running, add the dates, one at a time. Spread this mixture over the base of the tin and press it in evenly, pushing it right into the corners.

Repeat this process to make the cookie dough. Knead the dough together a little until it sticks well. Pull small pieces of the mixture apart and dot some of them sparsely over the base. Place in the freezer while you make the cream filling.

Place all the cream filling ingredients in a blender or food processor. Pulse to combine, then blend until super smooth. Pour a little over the base in the tin and spread evenly with a spatula. Add more of the cookie dough mixture as above. Repeat these steps until all the cookie dough and cream filling has been used.

Sprinkle the top of the slice with the crushed frozen raspberries and cacao nibs. Return to the freezer for a minimum of 4 hours to set.

Remove from the freezer 10 minutes before serving.

HEALTHY POPS 6 WAYS

On a hot day in summer, find delicious, pre-made treats in your freezer, created with whole, fresh ingredients that will nourish and cool you from the inside out. Here are some of my favourites.

PIÑA COLADA

Makes 8 × 100 ml (3½ fl oz)
   popsicles
Prep time: 15 minutes
   (+ 12 hours setting)

2 large apples
200 g (7 oz/2 cups) frozen pineapple
60 ml (2 fl oz/¼ cup) freshly squeezed
   lime juice
10 g (¼ oz/½ cup) fresh mint leaves

YOU WILL ALSO NEED
8 popsicle sticks
8 × 100 ml (3½ fl oz) popsicle moulds

Quarter the apples and feed them through a juicer. Transfer the juice to a blender, add the pineapple and lime juice and blend until evenly combined.

Divide the mint leaves between the moulds and pour the mixture on top. Use a popsicle stick to gently stir the mixture in the moulds so that the mint leaves are evenly distributed, then place a popsicle stick in each.

Place in the freezer to set for 12 hours or overnight. To remove from the moulds, let the pops stand for 2 minutes before gently lifting them out.

MANGO, PASSION & RASPBERRY

Makes 8 × 100 ml (3½ fl oz)
   popsicles
Prep time: 20 minutes
   (+ 12 hours setting)

5 mangoes, peeled and pitted
250 g (9 fl oz/1 cup) fresh passionfruit
   pulp
140 g (5 oz/1 cup) raspberries

YOU WILL ALSO NEED
8 popsicle sticks
8 × 100 ml (3½ fl oz) popsicle moulds

Blend the mango and passionfruit pulp until smooth. Pour half the mixture into the moulds and top each with a few raspberries. Pour the remaining mixture on top of the raspberries and stir each one to make sure there are no air gaps. Place a popsicle stick three-quarters of the way into each mould.

Place in the freezer to set for 12 hours or overnight. To remove from the moulds, partially fill a basin or sink with warm water, dip the moulds into the water for a few seconds, taking care not to fully submerge, then gently lift them out.

ROSE,
LEMONADE
& KIWI

Makes 8 × 100 ml (3½ fl oz)
  popsicles
Prep time: 10 minutes
  (+ 12 hours setting)

3 large apples
10 raspberries, fresh or frozen
1 tablespoon organic food-grade
  rosewater
170 g (6 oz/1 cup) kiwi fruit, peeled
  and sliced

Quarter the apples and feed
them through a juicer. Transfer
the juice to a blender, add the
raspberries and rosewater and
blend to combine.

Fill the moulds three-quarters
of the way and gently slide
two kiwi fruit slices into
each mould followed by a
popsicle stick.

Place in the freezer to set
for 12 hours or overnight. To
remove from the moulds, let the
pops stand for 2 minutes before
gently lifting them out.

CREAMY
LIME &
MAQUI BERRY

Makes 8 × 100 ml (3½ fl oz)
  popsicles
Prep time: 10 minutes
  (+ 12 hours setting)

LIME LAYER
80 ml (2½ fl oz/⅓ cup) freshly squeezed
  lime juice
80 ml (2½ fl oz/⅓ cup) maple syrup
2 medium avocados, peeled and
  stones removed

BERRY LAYER
1 mango, peeled and pitted
30 g (1 oz/¼ cup) mixed berries, fresh
  or frozen
2 teaspoons maqui berry powder
60 ml (2 fl oz/¼ cup) water

In a food processor or blender,
process all the lime layer
ingredients until super smooth.
Carefully fill each mould
halfway.

Repeat this process for
the berry layer, this time
filling to the top. Gently
push a popsicle stick
three-quarters of the way
into each mould, making sure
it is in the centre.

Place in the freezer to set
for 12 hours or overnight.
To remove from the moulds,
partially fill a basin or sink
with warm water, dip the
moulds into the water for a
few seconds (taking care not
to fully submerge them), then
gently lift them out.

GINGER, COCONUT & PEACH

Makes 8 × 100 ml (3½ fl oz)
  popsicles
Prep time: 20 minutes
  (+ 12 hours setting)

1 ripe peach, thinly sliced

CARAMEL GINGER
60 g (2 oz/¼ cup) Coconut yoghurt
  (page 144)
60 ml (2 fl oz/¼ cup) warm water
10 medjool dates, pitted
1 teaspoon finely grated fresh ginger

COCONUT
360 g (12½ oz/1½ cups) Coconut yoghurt
(page 144)
50 g (1¾ oz/¼ cup) coconut sugar
15 g (½ oz/¼ cup) desiccated (shredded)
  coconut
1 teaspoon finely grated fresh ginger

In a blender, pulse all the caramel ginger ingredients until smooth. Spoon into the bottom of your moulds.

Slide two slices of peach into the sides of each mould.

Blend all the coconut ingredients together, then pour into the top of the moulds. Place a popsicle stick three-quarters of the way into each mould.

Place in the freezer to set for 12 hours. To remove from the moulds, partially fill a basin or sink with warm water, dip the moulds into the water for a few seconds (taking care not to fully submerge them), then gently lift them out.

BLUEBERRY & VANILLA 'CHEESECAKE'

Makes 8 × 100 ml (3½ fl oz)
  popsicles
Prep time: 20 minutes
  (+ 24 hours soaking and setting)

FILLING
350 g (12½ oz/2½ cups) cashew nuts,
  soaked for 8 hours, drained and rinsed
125 ml (4 fl oz/½ cup) almond milk
80 ml (2½ fl oz/⅓ cup) maple syrup
60 ml (2 fl oz/¼ cup) freshly squeezed
  lime juice
½ teaspoon vanilla powder
130 g (4½ oz/1 cup) fresh blueberries

BASE
65 g (2¼ oz/½ cup) pistachio nuts
5 medjool dates, pitted

For the filling, blend the cashew nuts, almond milk, maple syrup, lime juice and vanilla powder together until smooth and creamy. Add the blueberries and pulse the mixture four to five times. Pour the mixture into popsicle moulds, leaving 2 cm (¾ in) at the top. Place a popsicle stick in each mould and place in the freezer to set for 12 hours or overnight.

Pulse the base ingredients until sticky and press into the top of the moulds. Return to the freezer for 4 hours or overnight. To remove from the moulds, partially fill a basin or sink with warm water, dip the moulds into the water for a few seconds (taking care not to fully submerge them), then gently lift them out.

RAW DESSERT BASICS

These raw dessert basics — a caramel date sauce, a cake base (page 116) and a chocolate (page 117) — make it easy to mix, match and build your own dessert creations. A few tips:

o Soak cashew nuts for 8 hours. This will help to produce a super smooth texture when blended.

o Make sure your dates are soft before you use them in cake bases and sauces, as they will blend more easily. If they are a bit firm, run them under warm water for a minute before blending.

o Use fruits and vegetables as healthy 'food dye'. Some good ones are turmeric, berries, English spinach juice and beetroot (beet) juice.

CARAMEL DATE SAUCE

Makes about 375 g (13 oz/1½ cups)
Prep time: 10 minutes

20 medjool dates, pitted

60 ml (2 fl oz/¼ cup) warm water

2 tablespoons coconut oil

1 teaspoon vanilla powder

2 pinches of quality mineral salt

In a high-speed blender or food processor, pulse all the ingredients to combine, then blend until super smooth and creamy. You may need to stop the motor every now and then to push the mixture down the sides so it combines evenly.

Serve a dollop with your favourite sweet dish, or spread over cakes.

CAKE BASE

Covers a 15 × 25 cm (6 × 10 in) slice tin
  or 18 cm (7 in) round cake tin

240 g (8½ oz/1½ cups) raw almonds
10 medjool dates, pitted

Blitz the almonds in a food processor for
5 seconds. Keeping the motor running,
add the dates, one at a time. Continue
blending until the mixture forms a sticky,
roughly textured dough.

Line a slice or cake tin and gently press
the mixture into the base until it is
entirely and evenly covered.

RAW CHOCOLATE

Makes about 790 g (1 lb 12 oz)
Prep time: 5 minutes
Cook time: 10 minutes

500 g (1 lb 2 oz) cacao butter, finely
   chopped or grated
140 g (5 oz/1 cup) cacao powder
125 ml (4 fl oz/½ cup) maple syrup

Gently melt the cacao butter in a double
boiler on low heat until a liquid forms.

Remove from the heat and add the cacao
powder and maple syrup. Whisk until no
lumps are left and the chocolate is
completely smooth.

The chocolate is now ready to pour into
moulds, drizzle over cakes or dunk a raw
cookie or energy ball into.

Place in the freezer to set it.

BASICS

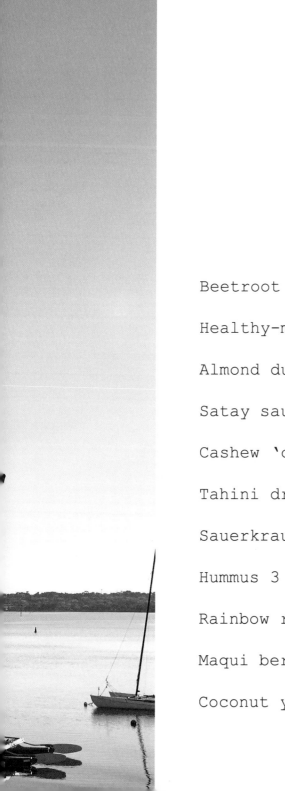

BEETROOT & DILL RELISH

Who can resist the magic combination of beetroot and dill? This relish is my nourishing alternative to the store-bought kind that is often laden with preservatives and white sugar. It makes a perfect, tasty little addition to veggie and mushroom burgers, avocado toast, roasted veggies or a yummy rainbow salad bowl. I like to make a big batch, as a jar-full always makes a very welcome gift too.

Makes 1–1½ kg (2 lb 3 oz–3 lb 5 oz/5–6 cups)
Prep time: 10 minutes
Cook time: 1 hour

1 kg (2 lb 3 oz) beetroot (beets), peeled and diced

3 medium green apples, peeled and diced

4 red onions, thinly sliced

300 g (10½ oz/1½ cups) coconut sugar

40 g (1½ oz/2 cups) fresh dill, finely chopped

250 ml (8½ fl oz/1 cup) apple-cider vinegar

Pulse the beetroot and apple in a food processor until finely chopped.

Combine the onion and coconut sugar in a saucepan and sauté for about 15 minutes over medium heat until all the sugar is dissolved and the onion is translucent and soft.

Increase the heat to high and add the beetroot and apple mix, dill and vinegar to the saucepan. Cook for 10 minutes, stirring well.

Place a lid on the saucepan, reduce the heat to low and simmer for 50 minutes, stirring occasionally.

Turn the stove off and allow the relish to cool for 30 minutes before dividing between warm, sterilised jars. Keep in the refrigerator for up to 2 weeks.

HEALTHY-MITE
SPREAD

Once you have tasted this easy-to-make, nutritionally dense version of that Aussie favourite, you will be hooked. It is super high in calcium, magnesium, iron and B12, and is made from only three ingredients. It's not hard to love something you can prepare in less than 5 minutes and have on hand for the next 8 weeks. Add to loads of delicious breakfasts, lunches and snacks.

Makes 250 g (9 oz/1 cup)
Prep time: 5 minutes

210 g (7½ oz/1½ cups) black sesame
  seeds
80 ml (2½ fl oz/⅓ cup) organic tamari
3 tablespoons nutritional yeast

In a high-speed blender, pulse all the ingredients to combine, then blend to a smooth paste.

Spoon the mixture into a sterilised jar. Store in the refrigerator and use within 8 weeks.

ALMOND DUKKAH

I have a batch of this delicious seasoning on hand at all times. It is the perfect addition to any savoury dish at breakfast, lunch or dinner. It is super easy to make and so versatile. Sprinkle in wraps, on salads and on avocado toast, stir into a yummy buckwheat pasta dish or use it to crumb a veggie burger. It is such a flavoursome addition. The sky's the limit.

Makes about 125 g (4½oz/1¼ cups)
Prep time: 5 minutes
Cook time: 20 minutes

160 g (5½ oz/1 cup) almonds
70 g (2½ oz/½ cup) sesame seeds
2 tablespoons whole cumin seeds
1 tablespoon coriander seeds
1 teaspoon whole peppercorns
1 teaspoon quality mineral salt

Heat a non-stick frying pan over medium heat. Add the almonds and stir for 10 minutes, or until lightly toasted. Spread the nuts on a plate to cool. Repeat this step with the sesame, cumin and coriander seeds, stirring until fragrant. Allow all the toasted nuts and seeds to cool to room temperature.

Combine the toasted nuts and seeds in a food processor with the peppercorns and salt. Pulse until evenly crushed.

Store in an airtight glass jar in a cool, dark place for 6—8 weeks.

SATAY SAUCE

You may have a bit of an 'I-can't-believe-this-is-good-for-you' moment when you taste this sauce, but I can assure you it is. Absolutely packed with healthy fats and protein, it can be used in so many different ways to 'yum-ify' a dish. You can use it as a salad dressing on loads of colourful raw veggies, dip fresh rice paper rolls into it, or even drizzle it over steamed greens with a little sprinkling of sesame seeds. Perfection.

Makes 250 g (9 oz/1 cup)
Prep time: 5 minutes

100 g (3½ oz) natural peanut butter

60 ml (2 fl oz/¼ cup) organic tamari

60 ml (2 fl oz/¼ cup) freshly squeezed
   lime juice

60 g (2 oz/⅓ cup) coconut sugar

3 garlic cloves, peeled

Blend all the ingredients together until smooth. Use within 2 days.

CASHEW 'CHEESE' 2 WAYS

GARLIC & CHIVE CASHEW CREAM 'CHEESE'

I am sure some cheese lovers would be pretty pleased to find out there is a super simple, plant-based, wholefood alternative that is oh-so scrumptious on any cracker. You can even modify this recipe and add your favourite herbs. I find dill and thyme both work really well. I love adding this to sandwiches, vegetable stacks and vegetable noodles, and spreading it thick on toast.

Makes 480 g (1 lb 1 oz/2 cups)
Prep time: 5 minutes
  (+ 8 hours soaking)

420 g (15 oz/3 cups) raw cashew nuts, soaked for 8 hours, drained and rinsed
125 ml (4 fl oz/½ cup) freshly squeezed lemon juice
3 tablespoons nutritional yeast
3 garlic cloves, peeled
1 teaspoon quality mineral salt
20 g (¾ oz/½ cup) fresh chives, chopped

Combine all the ingredients, except the chives, in a food processor and blend until smooth.

Stir in the chives and divide between sterilised jars. Store in the refrigerator for up to 2 weeks.

CASHEW 'PARMESAN'

This is one of those items I must have at the ready at all times. It only takes a couple of minutes to make, so it is never a hassle and it always adds that little bit of extra flavour to a salad, baked potato or even a zucchini (courgette) noodle dish. You can even try using other nuts, such as Brazil nuts, almonds, macadamia nuts or hazelnuts for different effects.

Makes 120 g (4½ oz/1 cup)
Prep time: 2 minutes

140 g (5 oz/1 cup) raw cashew nuts
20 g (¾ oz/¼ cup) nutritional yeast
1 teaspoon quality mineral salt

Add all the ingredients to a food processor and pulse until a grainy texture is achieved. Store in the refrigerator for up to 2 weeks.

TAHINI DRESSING
2 WAYS

These sweet and savoury dressings are my go-to creamy additions to many a dish. You don't need to spend ages shopping for a long list of ingredients to make the perfect dressing, and they are full of nutritional benefits.
I find the garlic version a great base to play with if you wish to add something unique to a dish. I like to make a batch at the beginning of the week to easily add to lunches and dinners on the go.

Makes about 375 g (13 oz/1½ cups)
Prep time: 5 minutes

GARLIC

80 g (2¾ oz) hulled tahini
80 ml (2½ fl oz/⅓ cup) almond milk
60 ml (2 fl oz/¼ cup) freshly squeezed
    lemon juice
2 teaspoons maple syrup
1 garlic clove, peeled

MINT

80 g (2¾ oz) hulled tahini
80 ml (2½ fl oz/⅓ cup) almond milk
60 ml (2 fl oz/¼ cup) freshly squeezed
    lemon juice
1 tablespoon maple syrup
10 g (¼ oz/½ cup) fresh mint leaves

Blend all the ingredients until smooth. Store in an airtight container in the refrigerator for up to 1 week.

SAUERKRAUT 2 WAYS

Sauerkraut (or sour cabbage) is, put simply, fermented cabbage. The health benefits of this traditional German side dish are amazing, including improving the digestive system, providing fibre and boosting immunity. It stores incredibly well in an airtight container in the refrigerator and is a healthy addition to any savoury dish. These two are my favourite sauerkraut flavours. I rarely eat a salad without a big spoonful of either.

Makes about 1 litre (34 fl oz/4 cups)
Prep time: 20 minutes (+ 5 days fermentation)

APPLE & DILL

1 large green cabbage, finely shredded,
   plus 2 large leaves
4 large green apples, peeled and grated
80 g (2¾ oz/¼ cup) quality sea salt
40 g (1½ oz/2 cups) fresh dill,
   finely chopped
3 tablespoons caraway seeds

BEETROOT & GINGER

1 large green cabbage, finely shredded,
   plus 2 large leaves
3 large beetroots (beets), peeled
   and grated
25 g (1 oz/¼ cup) quality mineral salt
1 tablespoon grated fresh ginger

Sterilise a chopping board, a sharp knife, a large mixing bowl, a wooden spoon and a large glass jar.

Remove the outer leaves of the cabbage and set two large leaves aside before shredding the rest and placing the shredded leaves in a large mixing bowl. Add all the other ingredients and massage firmly for approximately 10 minutes. Really squeeze the mixture in your hands as you go. A liquid should begin to form at the bottom of the bowl. This liquid should be almost level with the solids when you are finished massaging.

Cover and leave to rest for 1½ hours before scooping into a sterilised glass jar, leaving at least 3 cm (1¼ in) at the top. Place the two extra leaves over the mixture. Using a clean shot glass or other glass, gently push the cabbage leaves down until the brine rises over the mixture. Secure the lid and leave to ferment for approximately 5 days before storing in the refrigerator. It will keep for several months.

HUMMUS 3 WAYS

Hummus is my healthy, filling snack of choice. It is just perfect with sliced raw veggies or spread on a wrap with salad and falafels. It is also extremely simple to make and full of quality plant protein, calcium, fibre and healthy fats. These three are my favourites.

ROASTED GARLIC & ROSEMARY

Makes about 600 g (1 lb 5 oz/2 cups)
Prep time: 15 minutes
Cook time: 15 minutes

8–10 garlic cloves, peeled

4 fresh rosemary sprigs

500 g (1 lb 2 oz) tinned chickpeas, drained and rinsed

80 ml (2½ fl oz/⅓ cup) freshly squeezed lemon juice

100 g (3½ oz) hulled tahini

1 teaspoon quality mineral salt

TO SERVE

2 tablespoons olive oil (optional)

extra rosemary (optional)

Preheat the oven to 180°C (360°F) fan-forced.

Scatter the garlic and rosemary on a baking tray lined with baking paper and roast for 15 minutes, or until the garlic turns a golden colour. Leave to cool.

Scrape the rosemary leaves off the stem and discard the stem. In a food processor, pulse all the ingredients to combine, then blend until smooth. Spoon into a serving bowl, drizzle with olive oil and sprinkle with a little rosemary, if desired.

PAPRIKA & CAPSICUM

Makes about 600 g (1 lb 5 oz/2 cups)
Prep time: 15 minutes
Cook time: 25 minutes

2 red capsicums (bell peppers), halved
  and seeds removed
250 g (9 oz) tinned chickpeas, drained
  and rinsed
3 tablespoons hulled tahini
60 ml (2 fl oz/¼ cup) freshly squeezed
  lemon juice
1 tablespoon smoked paprika
3 garlic cloves
1 teaspoon quality mineral salt

TO SERVE
½ teaspoon smoked paprika
extra chickpeas (optional)

Preheat the oven to 200°C (390°F)
fan-forced.

Roast the capsicums on a baking tray lined
with baking paper for 25 minutes. Remove
from the oven and leave to cool.

In a food processor, pulse all the
ingredients to combine, then blend until
smooth. Sprinkle with the smoked paprika
and extra chickpeas, if desired, and
serve.

BEETROOT
& MINT

Makes about 450 g (1 lb/1½ cups)
Prep time: 15 minutes
Cook time: 30 minutes

3 large beetroot (beets) (approx. 600 g/
1 lb 5 oz), peeled and diced
250 g (9 oz) tinned chickpeas, drained
and rinsed
60 ml (2 fl oz/¼ cup) freshly squeezed
lemon juice
2 teaspoons grated lemon zest
2 tablespoons hulled tahini
2 garlic cloves, peeled
10 g (¼ oz/½ cup) fresh mint leaves
1½ teaspoons ground cumin
½ teaspoon quality mineral salt

TO SERVE
1 tablespoon Almond dukkah (page 126)
fresh mint leaves (optional)

Preheat the oven to 200°C (390°F)
fan-forced.

Spread the beetroot on a baking tray lined
with baking paper. Bake for 30 minutes.
Remove from the oven and leave to cool.

In a food processor, pulse all the
ingredients to combine, then blend until
smooth. Sprinkle with a little dukkah and
a few mint leaves, if desired, and serve.

RAINBOW RAW-NOLA

I just cannot go past this combination. I add it to so many summer breakfasts. It is especially nice when you scoop a bit into the bottom of your smoothie bowl before anything else, for a nice surprise at the end. You can even roll it into balls to snack on, or simply eat it as is.

Makes about 280 g (10 oz/2 cups)
Prep time: 5 minutes

80 g (2¾ oz/½ cup) activated buckwheat

65 g (2¼ oz/½ cup) pistachio nuts

60 g (2 oz/½ cup) dried goji berries

10 g (¼ oz/¼ cup) coconut flakes

6 medjool dates, pitted

½ teaspoon vanilla powder

TO SERVE
blueberries (optional)
green apple, sliced (optional)

Place all the ingredients in a food processor. Pulse ten to fifteen times until evenly combined and just beginning to stick together. Store in the refrigerator for up to 2 weeks. To serve, garnish with blueberries and sliced green apple, or other fruit, if desired.

MAQUI BERRY &
LIME CHIA JAM

You will hardly know that this jam is free from refined sugar, gelatin and preservatives when you taste it. The maqui berry gives it a delicious tart and sweet flavour while adding an abundance of antioxidants. I like to add it to my smoothie bowls, spread it on toast and hide it in delicious raw chocolate.

Makes about 600 g (1 lb 5 oz/2 cups)
Prep time: 5 minutes

130 g (4½ oz/2 cups) mixed berries, fresh or thawed from frozen
125 ml (4 fl oz/½ cup) maple syrup
60 ml (2 fl oz/¼ cup) freshly squeezed lemon juice
1 tablespoon maqui berry powder
½ teaspoon vanilla powder
85 g (3 oz/½ cup) white chia seeds

Blend the berries, maple syrup, lemon juice, maqui berry powder and vanilla powder until smooth. Pour the mixture into a bowl and stir in the chia seeds. Leave to stand for 10 minutes, then stir well again, making sure there are no clumps of chia. Pour into sterilised jars and let stand for 30 minutes before storing in the refrigerator.

COCONUT YOGHURT

Coconuts are a powerhouse of quality fats and are super gentle on digestion, so what better way to use them than to turn them into creamy and delicious probiotic yoghurt. Make sure you use quality organic coconut milk and cream, as this will make all the difference to the end result.

Makes 720 g (1 lb 9 oz/3 cups)
Prep time: 5 minutes

375 ml (12½ fl oz/1½ cups) full-fat
    coconut cream
375 ml (12½ fl oz/1½ cups) full-fat
    coconut milk
1 tablespoon maple syrup
2 dairy-free probiotic capsules

In a blender, combine the coconut cream, coconut milk and maple syrup. Pour into a bowl, sprinkle the contents of the capsules into the mixture and whisk to combine.

Divide the mixture between sterilised jars, resting the lids on top to allow air to circulate. Leave in a warm room (between 20–25°C/70–75°F) or place in an oven on the lowest setting for 24 hours. Stir the mixture after about 12 hours.

Once the yoghurt is fermented, seal the jars and refrigerate. The yoghurt will thicken a little more once chilled. If you would like a thicker, Greek-style yoghurt, substitute the coconut milk for more coconut cream and use only the thickened cream part, discarding the liquid.

AIR FRESHENER

BODY & HOME

TOOTHPASTE

There are many ingredients in conventional toothpastes that I would rather avoid. Thankfully there are inexpensive, easy-to-find ingredients that allow you to make your own. This is the simple recipe I use to make my toothpaste. It can take some getting used to, as the active ingredient can taste a little salty, but this toothpaste is a great natural alternative to commercial products. If you are after a sweeter version, simply add xylitol, which you can find at most health-food stores and online.

Makes about 120 g (4½ oz)
Prep time: 5 minutes

2 tablespoons melted coconut oil
20 drops organic food-grade
   peppermint essential oil
100 g (3½ oz) bicarbonate of soda
   (baking soda)
1 tablespoon xylitol icing
   (confectioners') sugar (optional)

YOU WILL ALSO NEED
a small glass jar

Melt the coconut oil in a double boiler. Add the peppermint oil, bicarbonate of soda and xylitol, if desired, and stir well to combine.

Store in an airtight glass jar.

To use, simply place about ¼ teaspoon of the mixture onto your toothbrush and use as normal.

DEODORANT

There is something so satisfying about creating your own products at home from natural ingredients and discovering that they not only work, they can cost a fraction of the price. These deodorant bars are a very good example of that. You can also have a play around with different topical essential oils to create your perfect scent, which is always fun.

Makes 2 × 100 ml (3½ fl oz) bars
Prep time: 5 minutes

100 g (3½ oz) cacao butter, shaved
  or grated
1 tablespoon coconut oil
2 tablespoons bicarbonate of soda
  (baking soda)
2 tablespoons arrowroot powder
5 drops lavender oil

YOU WILL ALSO NEED
silicone cupcake moulds or popsicle
  moulds

Gently melt the cacao butter in a double boiler. Stir in all the other ingredients, then pour the mixture into moulds.

Place in the refrigerator for 1 hour. Remove from the moulds and use as normal.

BODY SCRUB 2 WAYS

> Pampering your body with this shower ritual every now and then is so beneficial. Not only does your skin feel refreshed and smooth, there are many physiological benefits, including boosting circulation, and detoxifying and renewing skin cells. It is also a great way to use leftover coffee grounds.

Makes about 360 g (12½ oz/1½ cups)
Prep time: 5 minutes

MOCHA & VANILLA

100 g (3½ oz) raw sugar

3 tablespoons leftover coffee grounds, drained and cooled

3 tablespoons sea salt

2 tablespoons coconut sugar

2 tablespoons melted coconut oil

1 teaspoon vanilla powder

1 teaspoon cacao powder

PEPPERMINT & LEMONGRASS

100 ml (3½ fl oz) melted coconut oil

100 g (3½ oz) raw sugar

3 tablespoons sea salt

2 tablespoons coconut sugar

4 drops organic food-grade peppermint oil

2 drops organic food-grade lemongrass oil

Combine all the ingredients in a wide jar and mix well with a fork.

To use, gently rub onto wet skin in a circular motion once a week, avoiding the eyes. Rinse well and pat dry.

BATH SOAK

Bath soak is so easy to throw together and can be a lovely gift too. I like to add lavender for its calming qualities, so you can really sink in and enjoy. Indulging in a relaxing warm bath has many health benefits, including reducing blood pressure, improving blood circulation, clearing skin and aiding sleep. The Epsom salts (magnesium sulfate) are the star ingredient in this recipe, as soaking in them every now and then can aid in detoxification and help the body to absorb nutrients.

Makes about 190 g (6½ oz/1¼ cups)
Prep time: 5 minutes

200 g (7 oz/1 cup) Epsom salts
   (magnesium sulphate)
3 tablespoons sea salt
4 drops rose geranium oil
2 drops lavender oil

Combine all the ingredients in a glass jar and stir well with a fork.

To use, add a tablespoon to a warm running bath, relax and enjoy!

REPLENISHING FACE
& BODY MASK

This easy recipe is such a beautiful, nourishing ritual for your skin.
The avocado and coconut oil moisturise, while the lemon cleanses. I like
to make this every few months, especially in summer, to give my
skin some pampering.

Makes about 240 g (8½ oz/1 cup)
Prep time: 2 minutes

2 medium ripe avocados, stones removed

½ tablespoon coconut oil, melted

juice of 1 lemon

Spoon the avocado flesh into a blender or food processor. Add the coconut oil and lemon juice and blend until smooth and creamy.

To use, apply to clean, dry skin, avoiding the eyes and any sensitive areas. Leave for 10 minutes before washing off. Pat dry.

ALL-PURPOSE CLEANER

I don't know about you, but when I smell conventional cleaning products I don't exactly feel like breathing deeply. This simple recipe is made with affordable, easy-to-find ingredients that last and last. And the best bit? It is free from chemicals, not tested on animals, and it's kind to the environment and, of course, your health.

Makes 500 ml (17 fl oz/2 cups)
Prep time: 2 minutes

500 ml (17 fl oz/2 cups) white vinegar
2 teaspoons bicarbonate of soda
   (baking soda)
20 drops eucalyptus oil
5 drops lemongrass oil

YOU WILL NEED
500 ml (17 fl oz/2 cup) glass bottle
pump-action lid

Pour the vinegar into a glass bottle. Slowly add the bicarbonate of soda and then the essential oils. Secure the lid.

Shake before each use.

AIR FRESHENER

I believe air freshener should have a clean smell that lifts your mood. For these two easy air freshener recipes I use organic essential oils to recreate that crisp and clear smell of the great outdoors, naturally.

SPRAY

Makes 250 ml (8½ fl oz/1 cup)
Prep time: 2 minutes

250 ml (8½ fl oz/1 cup) purified water
20 drops lemongrass oil
15 drops eucalyptus oil
5 drops rose geranium oil

Combine all the ingredients in a sterilised glass spray bottle.

Shake before each use and use as normal.

DIFFUSER

Makes 100 g (3½ oz)
Prep time: 2 minutes

80 g (2¾ oz) bicarbonate of soda
  (baking soda)
40 drops lemongrass oil

Combine the bicarbonate of soda and the oil in a small glass jar and stir well.

Cut out a circle of paper 3–4 cm (1¼–1½ in) larger than the jar opening and secure around the lid with an elastic band or piece of string.

Using a pen or pencil, poke five or six holes in the paper.

When the diffuser begins to lose its smell, stir again and replace the lid.

Ingredients glossary

Acai berry

One of the richest natural sources of antioxidants, this berry has a strong purple colour and a subtle flavour. Organic acai is harvested deep within the Amazon. Look out for ethically sourced and certified organic varieties. It can be found in both freeze-dried powder form and frozen form in health-food stores and online.

Activated buckwheat

Activated buckwheat is made from the seeds of the buckwheat plant. Despite its name, buckwheat is not actually a grain but a small alkalising seed. The activating process, which involves soaking, washing and dehydration at low temperatures, makes the buckwheat easier to digest. You can find this crunchy breakfast food in your local health-food store, online and in some supermarkets.

Apple-cider vinegar

Raw apple-cider vinegar made with organically grown apples is cleansing, alkalising and energising. It adds flavour to salads and sauces, and can be taken diluted in water as a digestive aid before meals. Find it at your local health-food store, organic grocer and in some supermarkets.

Cacao butter

This is an edible fat extracted by first grinding the cacao bean to form a paste. The butter is then extracted from the paste. Cacao butter is the basis of all quality real chocolate. Full of antioxidants, it can be found in many health-food stores, organic grocers and online.

Cacao nibs

Another product of the cacao bean, like a healthy chocolate chip, the cacao nib is packed with antioxidants and magnesium. The nibs are a delicious addition to any smoothie bowl, trail mix or bliss bite and can be found in almost all health-food stores, online and at organic grocers.

Cacao powder

The raw form of cocoa powder and derived from the cacao bean, this powder is a nutritionally dense substance that can substitute the more conventional roasted cocoa powder. It can be added to many desserts and smoothies. This can be found in many health-food stores, online and some supermarkets.

Chia seeds

Chia seeds, an ancient seed native to Central America, have a mild nutty flavour and are high in healthy omega-3 fatty acids. They are often used as an egg substitute, as they expand when added to liquid to create a jelly-like texture. You can find them in health-food stores and supermarkets.

Coconut flakes

Coconut flakes, otherwise known as coconut chips, are dehydrated pieces of coconut flesh. Look out for sulphite-free fair-trade versions at organic grocers, health-food stores, online and in some supermarkets.

Coconut oil

Coconut oil is the edible oil extracted from coconut meat. It has a high smoking point, making it a great oil to cook with. It is also a wonderful, nourishing alternative to conventional beauty products. You can find it in the health-food aisle in supermarkets, in health-food stores and online.

Coconut sugar

Coconut sugar is made from evaporated coconut nectar from the blossom of the coconut palm. It has a delicious caramel flavour and a lower glycaemic index than sugar from the sugar cane, as well as more vitamins and minerals. Coconut sugar can be found in many health-food stores, online and now in many supermarkets.

Coconut water

Coconut water is the slightly sweet water derived from young green coconuts. It is full of electrolytes and can be found in many supermarkets, health-food stores and online.

Cold-drip coffee

Cold-drip coffee is a liquid made by filtering gravity-fed iced water through roasted and ground coffee beans. You can buy pre-made bottles from some organic cafes, health-food stores and organic grocers, as well as from quality coffee roasters.

Green supplement powder

Green supplement powders come in many forms and combinations. Sprirulina, chlorella and barley grass are common ingredients, and you can find these individually as well. Look for organic and sustainably sourced versions with no added preservatives or colourings. You will find a wide variety in health-food stores and online.

Maple syrup

I always use pure, organic Canadian maple syrup. Maple syrup is made from the sap of Canadian maple trees and holds a range of vitamins and minerals such as vitamin B6 and C. Real maple syrup can be found in most supermarkets, health-food stores, delicatessens and organic grocers.

Maqui berry powder

Maqui berries are known to be one of the highest antioxidant fruits on the planet. The powder is slightly tart and sweet, and makes a delicious addition to smoothies. It is a true beauty food and full of vibrant colour. The powdered form can be found in health-food stores and online.

Medjool dates

Harvested from the date palm, medjool dates are sweet and juicy even when dried. They are often larger than many other dates and full of fibre. They also contain high levels of essential minerals such as magnesium, copper, potassium and manganese. They are a great alternative to conventional cane sugar and provide a healthy source of energy. Medjool dates can easily be found in most supermarkets, organic grocers and in some health-food stores and delicatessens.

Mineral-rich salt

Some salts, depending on where they are harvested, can contain beneficial trace minerals such as potassium, iron and zinc. Good examples of mineral-rich salts are Himalayan pink sea salt, Klamath Krystal Salt and Celtic Sea Salt — I like to use Murray River Gourmet Salt. These can be found in delicatessens, organic grocers, some supermarkets, health-food stores and online.

Nutritional yeast

Nutritional yeast (also known as savoury yeast flakes) is an inactive yeast grown on molasses, then washed and dried with heat to deactivate it. It is a great source of vitamin B12, folic acid, selenium, zinc and protein. Nutritional yeast is typically used in plant-based cooking to add a cheesy, nutty, savoury flavour. It can be found in some health-food stores, organic grocers and online. Please note that nutritional yeast is completely different from brewer's yeast.

Orange essential oil

The essential oil derived from orange peel is a powerful anti-inflammatory. Be sure the brand you use in any food or drink is food-grade and certified organic. Only a tiny amount is needed because of its potency. You will find food-grade organic essential oils online and in some health-food stores.

Peppermint essential oil

Only a few drops of this essential oil, derived from the peppermint plant, provide an enormous amount of flavour in raw desserts and chocolates. If you are using peppermint oil in food or drink, you must make sure it is food-grade and certified organic. You can find it in some health-food stores and online.

Plant-based milk

Milk can be derived from some plants, seeds, grains and nuts. Some of the available plant-based milks are: oat milk, cashew milk, almond milk, rice milk, quinoa milk, macadamia milk and coconut milk. You can find many plant-based milk varieties in your local supermarket or health-food store.

Probiotic capsules

Dairy-free probiotic powders and capsules are widely available these days, and there are many different varieties. You can find these in pharmacies, some health-food stores and online.

Tahini

Tahini is a smooth, creamy, calcium-rich paste made from ground sesame seeds. Both hulled tahini and unhulled tahini are available. I have used hulled tahini in the recipes in this book. You can find both varieties in most larger supermarkets, health-food stores and online.

Tamari

Real, traditionally brewed tamari made from 100 per cent soy is naturally gluten-free. This unique and versatile Japanese seasoning is rich in vitamin B3 and makes a great substitute for salt and a tasty addition to sauces and salad dressings. You can find organic tamari in many health-food stores and organic grocers.

Vanilla powder

Vanilla powder or vanilla-bean powder is the ground powder from the vanilla bean. Make sure to look for certified organic varieties with no added cane sugar or preservatives. Vanilla powder can be found online and in some health-food stores.

Xylitol

Xylitol is typically used as a lower calorie substitute for sugar. It comes in a few forms. I do not use xylitol in cooking and raw, plant-based recipes, but it has shown to be beneficial for dental health and re-mineralisation – and with its sweet flavour, it makes a great addition to homemade natural toothpaste. I use the xylitol icing (confectioners') sugar in my toothpaste recipe on page 150. Many health-food stores carry this product.

Index

Acknowledgements

I must begin my mile-long list of people to thank with Natural Harry's better half, Fraser. Frase not only came up with the idea to build the Natural Harry caravan, but also actually designed and then constructed it from scratch. He has been an unwavering support from the very beginning, not to mention someone to laugh and share the long summer workdays with. He too has put his heart and soul into making Natural Harry the best it can be and, for that, I am not only in awe but truly grateful.

Next, I would like to thank Nikole Ramsay, my amazing photographer. This book would not look the way it does without her unique talent. Nikole was a constant support and positive influence in the development of this book and for that I cannot thank her enough.

Thank you to all of our friends, near and far, for recipe testing, lending a helping hand in the early days and just being all-round legends keeping Frase and I sane during the crazy summer. Thank you to the 'Jamon' crew who bravely taste-tested vegan treats more than three years ago. Thank you to Clare for your lesson in design and layout, and for joining me on surf and yoga breaks. This 'technophobe' would not have managed this without it. Thank you to Sophie, Amanda and Asho, who helped serve epic, ice-cold smoothies on sweltering summer days and were so much fun to be around. Thank you to Asho and Fliss for the constant laughs, always. I love you girls.

Thank you to Alice, aka She's a Wildflower, for her friendship, laughs and business meetings. Busy with her floristry business, she took time to moonlight at photoshoots as a self proclaimed prop-b**ch.

Thank you to my beautiful family, who believed in my 'hair-brained' desire to open a miniature outdoor cafe on wheels and produce 100 per cent organic, vegan smoothies and raw desserts. Especially to my amazing Mum, Sally, and Dad, John, who gave so much of their time that first summer and continue to be the solid foundation I am so lucky to have. I would also like to thank Fraser's parents, Debbie and Haydn, for being recipe testers and a constant support. Thank you to Haydn, who gave so much time and expertise in the building of the Natural Harry caravan.

I would like to say a heartfelt thank you to Suzie Mackenzie, Caroline Adams and Penny Cordner, who went to a huge effort to make sure my dyslexia didn't make it onto these pages.

Thank you to all of the Barwon Heads locals who believed in us from the beginning and welcomed something a bit different to the main street.

A big thank you has to go to Angie and Mel at Organic Mojo for supplying Natural Harry with its juicy organic goodness. These two hilarious characters made fumbling through the first few weeks a hoot. Plus, you have to respect someone who gets up at 3 am twice a week to bring you organic fruit and veg.

Thank you to all our Instagram and Facebook followers, email subscribers and the wider Geelong community, amazing cafes and stockists who have always supported us.

Finally, a very big thank you to all of our Natural Harry customers for giving Natural Harry its life and filling the space with laughter and good vibes. Thank you for believing in us and helping to nurture the organic farming industry, the environment and your body.

X Harry

Oven temperatures are for fan-forced ovens. If you have a conventional oven, increase the
temperature by 20°C (70°F).

This book uses 20 ml (¾ fl oz) tablespoons. Cooks using 15 ml (½ fl oz) tablespoons should be generous
with their tablespoon measurements. Metric cup measurements are used, i.e., 250 ml (8½ fl oz) for
1 cup. In the US a cup is 237 ml (8 fl oz), so American cooks should be generous with their cup
measurements; in the UK, a cup is 284 ml (9½ fl oz), so British cooks should be scant.

This edition published in 2021 by Hardie Grant Books, an imprint of Hardie Grant Publishing
First published in 2015 by Harriet Birrell

Hardie Grant Books (Melbourne)
Wurundjeri Country
Building 1, 658 Church Street
Richmond, Victoria 3121

Hardie Grant Books (London)
5th & 6th Floors
52–54 Southwark Street
London SE1 1UN

hardiegrantbooks.com

 A catalogue record for this
book is available from the
National Library of Australia

Natural Harry
978 1 74379 789 1

10 9 8 7 6 5 4 3 2

Publishing Director: Jane Willson
Project Editor: Loran McDougall
Editors: Harriet Birrell and Ariana Klepac
Designer: Harriet Birrell
Photographer: Nikole Ramsay
Production Manager: Todd Rechner

Colour reproduction by Splitting Image Colour Studio
Printed in China by Leo Paper Products LTD.

Hardie Grant acknowledges the Traditional Owners of the country on which we work, the
Wurundjeri people of the Kulin nation and the Gadigal people of the Eora nation, and recognises
their continuing connection to the land, waters and culture. We pay our respects to their Elders
past, present and emerging.

Disclaimer The use of this book is at the sole risk of the reader. Its content does not replace medical
advice and is not a substitution for a physician's advice for, or diagnosis of, any health issue. The
information contained herein is general and may not be suitable for everyone. For your safety, follow
the guidelines in this book. The publisher makes no guarantee as to the effects of the recipes and
no liability will be accepted. To the maximum permitted by law, the author and publisher exclude all
liability to any person arising directly or indirectly from using this book.

 The paper this book is printed on is from FSC®-certified forests and other
sources. FSC® promotes environmentally responsible, socially beneficial and
economically viable management of the world's forests